Long Line Rider

Also by Gladys Iris Clark

Forever Young

Long Line Rider

The 1893 opening of the Cherokee Strip

Gladys Iris Crouch Clark

Edited by

Carmelita Clark Headland
and
Astrid Gallagher

Formatted by

Stephen Clark Headland

Cover design by Ayse Nur Ataysoy is based on the 10 ft by 60 ft. mural, *Oklahoma Land Rush, Alva, Ok*. Image used by permission of the Alva Historical Society.

Long Line Rider is dedicated to those pioneers, their families and descendants who stayed the course in the Outlet through the worst and best of times.

TABLE OF CONTENTS

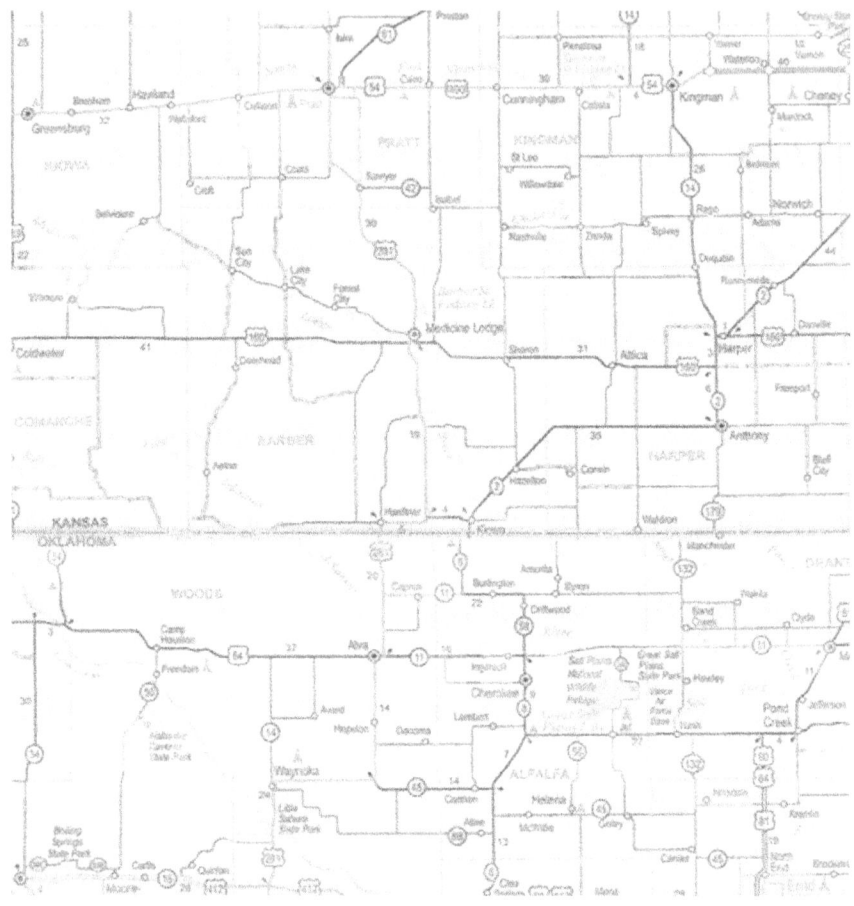

Current map of the Kansas-Oklahoma border area, showing US Highway 281 from Pratt, KS to Alva, OK.

INTRODUCTION

Buffalo and antelope roamed the high plains of the North American Continent. Men seeking new lands gradually moved westward, conquering the continent. The buffalo were a satisfying source of meat and the hides brought quick revenue on the eastern markets. The buffalo hunters slaughtered the American bison and the thundering herds fell in their tracks. Only the dry chips remained to fuel fires for the drovers of longhorns as they crossed the plains northward to cattle markets. After 1869, when the railroads crossed the continent and the cattle were shipped by rail the Western Trail was abandoned.

Several huge cattle outfits freely grazed the tens of thousands of acres of government land that earlier had been reserved for the Cherokee Nation as an outlet to their hunting grounds. A range war erupted between rival cattlemen, so the government ordered everyone and their herds off the Outlet. Responding to demands from protesters against allowing only Indians to possess land in Oklahoma Territory, the government arranged to open up the Cherokee Outlet in the northwestern section of Oklahoma Territory to white homesteaders. This was to be the last race for free land; thereafter the government arranged for auctions and drawings for homesteads and lots. The greatest land run took place in 1893 and is remembered as the largest and most spectacular race in the annals of American history.

Virgin Soil

As long as the prairie creek flows and the
Autumn sun lengthens its shadow mass,
When the sod furrows turn back to seed
And the dust bowl turns to grass--
As long as the purple sage blooms, and
With life's chores I come to grip,
Then do I escape the present and
Remember the Cherokee Strip

***

Gladys Iris Crouch Clark

CHAPTER 1

THE LONG LINE

A thick cloud of ochre-colored dust hung obstinately along the border between Kansas and Oklahoma Territory for two hundred and twenty-six miles. Along that invisible border a temporary line of hopeful homesteaders marked the starting front for participants of the most stupendous Race any government ever arranged. The total prize was forty thousand quarter sections of free prairie land of one hundred and sixty acres each. Over one hundred thousand entrants formed the long line.

At high noon on September 16th, 1893, four hundred riflemen stationed within earshot of each other, carbines at the ready, would signal the start of the long awaited Race into the Cherokee Strip for free homesteads. The size of the rectangle of land was enormous. The six million acres covered an area as large as three eastern states put together, Connecticut, Rhode Island and Delaware.

People came from everywhere, some arriving days in advance to participate, while others came to witness a never-to-be-repeated occasion. Still others came to peddle their wares. William S. Prettyman, one of the photographers who was on hand, became famous because of his pictures taken at the start of the Race. Every imaginable vehicle, pulled by every imaginable kind of beast, including horses, mules, burros and oxen entered the starting line, where even bicycles had a trial.

Sweat, grime and insects irritated the waiting throng and their steeds. Most rode horses for a quicker get-away. The carriage crowd was there too, along with tenderfeet from the eastern seaboard riding livery stable sprinters or rented rigs. The Rock Island and Santa Fe railroads had special coaches filled to capacity with eager challengers. Several stagecoaches were pressed into service, each with its share of customers, some waving their permits purchased from the several land agents in small portable huts.

1

The weather could have been worse so close to the autumnal equinox when dust storms usually preceded rains, but only the occasional dust devil annoyed the participants waiting in line. The stinging bites of the pesky green flies and the constant tail swishing of the horses irritated them as well. No wonder the motley throng displayed taut nerves in outbursts of undisciplined tempers. Not everyone showed a bad frame of mind as some were whooping it up. After all, this was a special day of celebration for those killing time by lifting the little brown jug to their lips in the many tent saloons set up behind the lines.

A milling crowd trod uneasily behind the restless horses who were as unpredictable as their riders. The horses stamped continuously, the dust rising relentlessly. The combined sounds of buzzing flies and stamping hooves and overwhelming odors gave reality to the scene. The dusty haze overshadowed man and beast until the sun was barely visible. For those who had been standing at their post since dawn, determined not to be left behind, the appointed time couldn't come too soon.

The Cherokee Strip, also known as the Outlet by the range riders of the huge cattle enterprises and by the drovers of The Western Trail, actually had been set aside for the Indians to cross over to their hunting grounds in the west. After the buffalo virtually disappeared there was no more use for the Outlet. Cattle grazed free until the chief of one tribe accepted a considerable fee for the use of his grazing land without government approval. Other tribes protested and eventually a range war ensued. To put an end to this and to another complaint by a group called the Boomers, who claimed the government discriminated against white settlers in allotting most of Oklahoma Territory to the Indians, President Grover Cleveland signed The Free Lands Act in 1890. The railroads and the tradesmen were jubilant. So were the hopefuls who had missed the 1889 Race to the Cimarron River, which included the rich counties where Oklahoma City and Guthrie were located. The Outlet would offer great chunks of virgin land to those future homesteaders able to grab a piece.

Down near the west end of the line where there were fewer vehicles and more room, a long string of riders waited expectantly as if glued to their mounts and looking like centaurs ready to leap into the unknown. One of these hopefuls was a rider named Jim Crouch. After the misery of the Civil War when Jim was a lad of fifteen, he and his older brother Keene had ridden west from their father's Kentucky plantation. A year later, after a few months of schooling at Ottawa, Kansas, where an uncle had settled, Jim joined an outfit that drove longhorns from Vernon, Texas to Dodge City, Kansas. Herding cattle became his profession. Those long drives lasted until the railroads came. Drovers then found work with the cattle barons who grazed vast herds on government land. Jim became a range rider in the Outlet and in No Man's Land also known as the Oklahoma Panhandle.

When the government ordered all cattle removed from the Outlet, Jim realized his days of cattle punching were coming to an end. Though he knew little of farming, he could see his future lay in owning his own land.

Jim Crouch looked younger than his twenty-nine years despite having worked hard outdoors. His dark hair framed a gentle visage and his sky-blue eyes looked ahead with determination. For years Jim had evaded the enticing charms of the ladies until he met the handsome dark-eyed Elizabeth Bevis, whom everybody called Lizzie. The instant attraction was double-barreled love, and soon they were hitched and working in double harness. A year later their son Robbie was born.

Jim thought of Lizzie's confidence, now four months pregnant with their second child, camped back of the line together with their son Robbie, her father and her brother Ott. There was no doubt in Jim's mind that he would find his chosen quarter section, stake his claim, and dig a sod dugout in time for the babe's entrance into the world.

Jim tied a bandanna over his mouth in an effort to keep some of the dust out of his lungs. A grizzled middle aged codger swung his buckskin cayuse[1] into the narrow space at Jim's left, eyeing him as if he were some sort of bandit. The stranger looked lean and lanky and somewhat undernourished, as did his horse. In an instant each had sized up the other fellow.

"Well, fer crimminy sakes!" said the stranger to Jim. "Who ever woulda believed that an old down and outer like me with an old plug like mine would be nestled up to a sleek young hoss like that one you're ridin'? Say, he's a dandy. You musta got him up North from one of them Indian tribes where those speckled rumps come from."

"Hardly," Jim answered. "But guess his sire did come from up there. I suspect he has a strain of Morgan and some thoroughbred racing stock in him too. I raised him from a foal."

"To change the subject," Jim remarked, "what I want to hear now is the crack of the rifles."

"What time is it, I wonder?" The stranger asked.

Jim, tolerant of most men and beasts, except for a kind of dude-show-off, smiled broadly. Then he took out his watch and fob.

"Let's see," Jim replied, "according to railroad time it is eleven fifteen. We've got forty-five minutes left and it's going to take some doing to keep Barney quiet. This horse likes the open prairie. Crowds make him nervous, cooped up like this."

A youthful rider astride a sorrel pony, both of them panting and looking bedraggled, managed to slip in on Jim's right.

"Well, I made it after all, fer jimminy sakes! Almost feared I'd never find a space, ridin' fer days like I have. But I got my permit all right and can't give up now," the pony rider said. He dismounted and put a feed-bag to the poor critter while the other men looked on. "Sorry fellas," he added, "but if this nag don't get some oats she'll never finish the race. Hope it don't upset your animals. There's only a couple of handfuls left anyway. I've come

---

1 Cayuse: Although settlers called most horses raised by the American Indians "cayuse ponies," the little known Cayuse Indian Pony of the Northwest is a distinct breed which originated in the 1800s. Its conformation and its background set it apart from the mustang, Spanish Barb, or other wild horses.

all the way from Ioway and it took an extra day fer grazing to give her enough stamina to make the trip. How long you fellas been awaitin'?"

"Say," Jim answered, ignoring the question, "since we're going to be standing here together you might as well know my name is Crouch. Jim Crouch, drover, buffalo skinner, sometime cook, and all around wrangler. From now on I expect to be a homesteader."

Then he turned to the first stranger who was wearing an old sleek fringed jacket of deer hide, ripped down a ways in the back seam.

"Call me Josh," the old-timer stammered. "Josh Montgomery is my name."

"Here I'm fergettin' my manners already," said the pony rider. "I'm Henry Hartner but no one calls me Heny or Henry. I'm just Hank to everybody."

"I jist got here ahead of you," Josh said. "But Crouch here, from the looks of him, knows a heap about where he's a headin'. We might be smart to follow his lead. That right, Jim?"

"How about yourself, Josh?" Jim queried. "You look like you know the prairie as well as I do. But I will admit I've been in these parts before. You can follow me if you think you can keep up but if you lose me, I'll be veering slightly left, after crossing the Salt Fork, probably a dried up stream this time of the year," Jim said compassionately. He thought he might as well steer these poor men straight.

"That's right friendly of you, sir," Hank said. "I appreciate your advice, but right now I'm dead sleepy and my nag needs rest, too, these few minutes we got left." He took a few dried apricots out of his jacket offering them around.

Josh accepted one, but Jim declined. Before the young man had time to chew it, he fell asleep leaning against his pony. The other two kept talking.

"Wish I'd made the Cimarron run in '89," Josh said. "It gets more rain further east than this dried up prairie does."

"Why in hades didn't you?" Jim said in an annoyed tone "You mighta had a stake in Oklahoma City or Guthrie by now. I hear those cities are getting mighty populated."

"Couldn't," Josh replied. "I was holed-in over in No Man's Land. Had to clear out of Indian Territory. Scared I'd get taken in fer rum runnin'."

"That's a coincidence," Jim said. "I've spent a good deal of the time there myself but I was riding the range for a cattle outfit. Saw outlaws and bandits but they looked just like us and you couldn't tell us apart, as far as behavior is concerned. Most acted pretty straight."

The minutes were ticking away. The dust grew worse as more hooves tore up the turf. The noise abated some but the tension increased. Each participant had but one idea that filled the atmosphere like a selfish force, to beat everyone else if he could. Even Jim Crouch, usually more considerate of others than of himself, became strangely susceptible. His plan was to win. Once the race began he would stop for no man or obstacle, baring any unforeseen event.

"My half-brother Charley," Josh said. "He was my only kin, younger by far than me, almost like a son. If he had hid out with me there, he would be alive today,"

"What's that you said happened to your brother?" Hank woke from his catnap with a start.

"I was jist tellin' Crouch here that I lost my only kin a few years back while I was holed-in over in No Man's Land," Josh repeated. "A bullet from the gun of that dastardly outlaw, Bob Dalton, killed Charley. He shot him in the back before he had a chance to draw. Dalton was wearin' a deputy's badge then but he sure lost it on account of it. Trigger-happy he was. He claimed Charley was tryin' to steal a horse from a rich man's barn. The truth came out that my brother had been workin' for this rancher and only returned to get his duffel bag a'clothes. At stake was Dalton's pride. His girl Minnie was sweet on Charley so he had a lookout named Sharkey that tipped him off."

"That's a dirty shame. Thought I heard the Daltons were dead," Hank commented.

"You're right about that, Hank," Josh said. "I heard most of them were killed in a bank robbery and are rottin' over in the Coffeyville cemetery. That's where Charley is buried too but I'll bet he don't need their company."

"Well, at least there is no use holding vengeance for Bob Dalton with him under the sod, is there?" Jim said.

"Not fer him, but Sharkey is jist as guilty, and someday I'm goin' to meet up with him." Josh's tone was adamant.

Some of the riders acted tanked up, and one cowboy offered Hank a swig from a hip pocket flask. "I ain't got no bad habits like that yet," he refused politely.

"Did you ever see the time linger on so slow?" Jim inquired.

"No, never!" Josh said. "How that fancy high-spirited hoss you're on, Jim, keeps from leapin' this line is a wonder. But he can't help stompin' which ain't good fer his shoes, I'd suppose. How come you know this prairie so well, Crouch?" Josh added.

Jim realized if they kept on talking the time would pass more quickly and perhaps relieve some of the strain of waiting. He patted Barney's neck and spoke quietly to him, calming him down before he answered Josh's question.

"When I first saw the Cherokee Strip, I was further to the west, closer to the Panhandle. There were plenty of buffalo left and I saw a migration of them and the antelope too, miles of them. But the part I'm heading for I saw on my last cattle drive before I started riding the range. It left an indelible impression on my memory."

"Guess we're in luck, Hank, to find a wrangler that knows the ropes here in the Outlet." Josh said.

"Speakin' of luck, I wish I knew I had it," answered Hank.

"Me too. I can tell this fella here has it," said Josh pointing to Jim. "If this worn-out cayuse had the go-gettedness he had when I went into No Man's Land a few years back, I'd have more faith."

"You all will make it, you'll see." Jim assured them.

"Only time will tell," Josh added. "Chances are we'll never see each other agin in this crowd of a hundred thousand or more. But if we should meet up agin let's remember what we said about luck."

"Luck is something you have to make for yourself," Jim said. "Work to cause it to happen and don't expect it to be bestowed on you for nothing. It's a combination of work and faith, a law of living, a game of give and take."

"Take this nag of mine," Hank said. "It was a Christmas present from my father when I was a boy in knee britches. Bein' a married man now with a wife in the family way, I'd think it's my bad luck that workin' all those years without wages, that my father coulda give me another horse for this race? Maybe he didn't want me to win so I'd stay on the farm with him."

"Could be," Jim commented. "Some fathers are like that. It doesn't dawn on them that some like to get out on their own, try their wings and fly away. But in the end you probably will get the farm."

"Not all of it, Jim. I got a brother and sisters."

Just then some smart alec blew into a paper sack and popped it. It sounded like the signal to those standing nearby and a few horses bolted. The militia guarding the line against such contingencies turned them back, yelling "false alarm!"

Another commotion behind them occurred when Ott Bevis, Jim's fourteen year-old brother-in-law forced his horse through the crowded line. "Hey Jim!" Ott shouted. "Thought I'd never find you. I brought somethin' for you and Barney." Ott dismounted carrying a gunnysack, dragging like it was almost empty. He left the reins down and the pony stood still.

"Pa said to give you some of this cracking corn[2] and some extra grain for Barney. It don't weigh much and the grazin's not much good where you're goin'. Lizzie put in a snack for you, too."

"Guess Barney will be pretty glad, but Ott, we can't use the sack," Jim said as he dismounted and untied his bedroll. He helped

---

2 Colloquial for Popcorn.

Ott put the grain and corn inside and Jim put Lizzie's food in his jacket pocket. "Can't have anything swinging from Barney's flanks on a ride like this."

Jim was about to swing back in the saddle when he thought of something. He took the tapaderos[3] off the stirrups to lessen the weight.

"Ott, carry these back so Lizzie can take care of them. There isn't much dense brush in these parts anyway. Won't need them."

"Okay, so long, Jim," Ott said. "Good luck! Oh, I most forgot. Here's some lucky Horseshoe plug tobacco."

Ott mounted his paint pony and headed back to their campsite. He looked handsome and sat straight on the horse blanket, reminding Jim of some young Indian bucks he had seen. He recalled that the boy had Indian blood. Not much, but Lizzie had said their father was one-eighth Powhatan. Funny, he thought, definitely a throwback.

Jim cinched up the saddle straps, looked at Barney's hooves and examined the lightweight horseshoes made especially for the race. He felt satisfied, mounting for the last time prior to the start.

"Well, it won't be a long wait from now on," Jim remarked as he looked at his watch. "Got only sixteen minutes before we take off and trample all the sagebrush down between us and a prairie paradise."

"Jim, you sure are countin' prairie chickens before they're hatched, ain't ya? What if ya couldn't locate a claim?" Josh asked.

"I'm not even doubting," Jim answered. "I just feel in my bones that I can't lose. I've been planning for this race ever since the Government announced it two years ago. Quit riding then 'cause the cattle outfits and their herds were ordered off the Strip so the surveyors could come in."

Jim reached in his pocket and found the plug of tobacco. Hank refused when it was offered, but Josh, who had been eyeing it greedily, took out a knife as big as a Bowie[4] and cut off an ample slice.

---

3 Tapaderos are leather stirrup covers that protect the boots in brushy areas.

4 A large fixed blade knife made famous by Jim Bowie.

"Well, call that my first piece of luck!" Josh said. "Just been wishin' I had a chaw, keeps my consarned mouth from gittin' so dry and it's a big aid to help me concentrate on what I'm doin'. Ain't you goin' to have a chaw, Jim?"

"No, I prefer a pipe. Don't think the dust I'm breathing would mix very well with the smoke. I sometimes chew a little tobacco when I'm riding the ranges just to be doing something, but not often." Jim thought about his brother-in-law. "Ott is a right smart young-un. He knew there weren't any stores for a distance of twelve miles or so from here, and no place to get stuff except from these tin-pan peddlers that ask three prices for things, and he thought ahead to give me something for the race. He'll be coming down to help me plow the sod when we get started."

Hank said that peddlers didn't come to faraway places like their Iowa farm because it was almost self sufficient in growing everything except pots and pans or soda and vanilla. "Jim, have you ever done much farmin'? Bein' around stock all your life bet you never thought you'd end up bein' a wheat farmer. Everyone else on this line sees the Cherokee Strip as fit for raisin' wheat I guess, unless they expect to sell their claim when they get it registered, if there's any buyers."

"Say, Crouch," Josh said, "moonshine is what peddlers make the most money on. Don't think that most of them don't have it. Charley and me did right smart with our set-up, coulda gotten rich if we'da had any sense. Guess I enjoyed the stuff too much, myself. We put in a false bottom to the spring wagon where we kept the hooch, covered it with a little straw where we kept a crate of chickens, a pail of lard, dried apples, spices and the lot. No revenooer ever got hep. Sometimes we jist used straight old white lightning, colored it with caramel or part wine then gave it a squirt of glycerin, and you woulda thought it was ten year old Kentucky bourbon."

"I'da thought that would be a threat to your freedom, livin' in the face of the law," Hank said.

The tone of the throng became lower as if they were cupping their ears for the signal. The hush and the noise came intermittently.

"Jim, you must be Irish to give your horse the name of Barney," Josh commented.

"No, not altogether," Jim answered. "I'm a mixture of Scotch-Irish and Welsh. I named Barney that because he was foaled in a barn, a distinction in itself."

"Guess I got off the subject," Josh said. "Wanted you to know why I took off to No Man's Land. One night at a honky-tonk, old demon rum loosed my tongue and I started braggin' to the little tart Charley was with. She took me aside and told me a Federal was listenin' to every word I said. I knew I'd spilled enough to get a long stretch so I high-tailed it."

When Josh finished talking, Jim took a look at his watch and put his finger to his lips for quiet. "Get ready fellas," he said. "It's time!"

A few seconds later a loud shot rang out! In fact four hundred shots, sounding as one, and the line of one hundred thousand hopeful homesteaders exploded in a flash.

CHAPTER 2

THE RACE

At the crack of the rifles Jim dug his spurs into his horse's flanks and Barney leaped forward with a mighty thrust of his pent-up energy. High-flying hooves thundered down the dry prairie and the earth shuddered under thousands of hoof-beats. Barney, his long white mane flying in the wind, nostrils dilated, shot into the lead, running free of the dust clouds behind.

The greatest race with the longest starting line ever assembled was off to an instant thrust, leaving vehicles that became entangled in harness or sideswiped by heavier wagons. An eyewitness, repelled at the tragedies he saw, left the scene in utter dismay, realizing that every entrant of the race cared little of what became of the next fellow. The militia and the few remaining onlookers rushed out to give aid and comfort to the victims of the crush. Numerous injuries and even some deaths resulted from being trampled. Sooners[1] had set fire to some parts of the prairie to prevent riders from overrunning their illegal stakes and claims. Greed and selfishness had a field day.

Jim didn't look back. His whole attention was on getting out in front and staying there. He let Barney run free for a spell to relieve his energy, but soon reined him in and held him to a steady ground-covering pace.

Flakes of thistledown filled the air and occasionally Jim found himself sneezing. This was more acceptable than the dust he had been breathing while waiting in line. The wind was in his favor. He noticed a few clouds gathering, which would be a relief from the heat if they didn't foretell a storm. Barney avoided clumps of wild gourds, knowing instinctively that rattlesnakes seek such shelter. Barney was a cautious animal. With his long stride his gait would have been faster were it not for the prairie dog mounds. Jim trusted Barney's native intelligence as much as his own.

---

1 Sooners were would-be settlers who entered government lands before the official starting date in order to stake a claim without enduring the waiting and the Race.

Despite the rapid pace they were traveling, Jim had time to muse on some of the sights and sounds he had observed while waiting. He was amazed at the variety of vehicles. Along with the usual wagons, buggies, surreys and the like, he remembered a woman seated in a sulky with the reins held high in her hands, ready to start. "What if the trotter doesn't break his stride to gallop?" Jim wondered. He recalled that his own sister-in-law, Vena, was supposed to be riding somewhere in this same race against her father's permission. She had entered the race despite his anger and the risk of a family break. He smiled when he thought of one of the Boomers going around ringing a cowbell saying, "We done it. This race wouldn't-a gotten anywhere without us Boomers." Jim knew he was telling the truth so he had yelled, "that's for sure!"

As the wind changed now and then, Jim heard the force of the riders coming at his rear. The sound and vibration were as great as a freight train. As smooth sailing as he had had so far, Jim was not about to let his caution down. He realized that there might be obstacles ahead in finding the benchmark, holding down the claim once he had driven in his stake, and most importantly in getting the claim registered. Meanwhile he was racing free as the wind and loving every moment.

Looking sideways to the east, a bunch of riders were parallel with him. Then he glanced to the west and saw several others coming close. He wondered if Barney was getting tired. First he would watch their pace before giving Barney the spurs. Like all cowboys Jim wore spurs but seldom used them. His steeds had spirit enough to go as fast as he wanted.

The prairie was full of game of the smaller variety. Only occasionally did they scare up a coyote, a homesteader's worst enemy, especially where there were chickens. The deer preferred a different diet and so were scarce in these parts. Jackrabbits and cottontails were everywhere. Barney veered over a thicket to avoid a foxhole and a coyote jumped out so fast that the horse almost unseated Jim. "You dastardly critter, you've had this prairie all to yourself so long you think it's yours, but from now on you're going to share it with us homesteaders. You varmints!" Jim cussed, shaking his fist.

The pace eased off a bit but not enough to slow down. It was obvious that the other steeds in contention were getting tired or winded. The open prairie before Jim beckoned like a magnet. Nature here could be cruel in its opposite seasons, its wet and dry spells. Yet even with the windstorms this was a land he thought he could tame. The meadowlarks stopped their melodious chirp, and took to their wings in sudden flight as Jim and Barney approached. Sparrows did also. Only the crows and the buzzards stood long enough to see what kind of enemy threatened before lifting up their wide black wings. The heat of midday had given way to more clouds in the sky shading the sun at intervals, which was a blessing. In sharp contrast to the pounding of hooves behind him, Jim invaded the stillness. He was ecstatic with the ride, feeling a lightness and a sense of weightlessness. Barney seemed to capture the spirit like a re-born Pegasus.

Jim mused with nostalgia about his early days, dreaming of the herds of buffalo and antelope he had seen on the high plains, and those he had shot for meat and hides. He treasured those hides he still had that he'd tanned himself. He reflected on the Indians' careful use of the buffalo herds. He had always respected their concern for nature's resources for it coincided with his own understanding of a living environment. There was no time to look at his watch but like most individuals in the West, he could look at the sun and instinctively come to a few minutes of the correct time of day.

"It must be almost three," he concluded out loud.

Jim, having ridden the lonely range for so long, had acquired the habit of talking to his mounts and even to himself. It helped pass the time and made him feel less isolated.

"It's just as I expected, Barney. We haven't seen nary a one of those sleek, curried livery stable steeds and their dudes pass us yet. It takes a working horse like you with strong legs and sure-footed caution to clip it off across the prairie and arrive ahead of the pack." Barney snorted as if he knew he was being praised.

As Jim rode through patches of jimson weed and poisonous nightshade he smelled their acrid odor. He knew he would have to eliminate them in the pastures where his stock would graze. He had seen both cattle and horses go loco after eating those pesky weeds.

His stock would be too precious for that. The hard little black seeds on the nightshade, when ripe were supposedly used medicinally to bring relief to the chest and stomach, but he wasn't sure. He knew exterminating them would be a big job.

Now and then tumbleweed rolled along beside him. The wind changed, whirlwinds engulfed them, then twisted off in vacant space. Jim called them dust devils, but he knew that on a larger scale they could be cyclonic. He rode out of the last one in which he couldn't see a thing in front of him and could barely hear the galloping hooves behind him.

Like most outdoorsmen Jim was philosophic and hated routine. He wondered if he was suited to settle down on one hundred and sixty acres with fences when he was used to whole territories without barriers of any kind. His rambling mind took him back to the Orphan Strip as some called No Man's Land where he had access to the whole Panhandle. Just being there, riding, roping and working the stock on the freest land on earth made his whole body tingle. He had wondered at the time if every man he met might be some bandit or outlaw claiming a haven from punishment or from extradition for infractions of the law committed elsewhere. He thought of Josh Montgomery whom he had just met at the starting line, certainly not a bad guy like most hideouts but admittedly a rumrunner, which was a federal offense. He remembered clearly the time nine years before when he and another rider, Tom Miller, had camped on a branch of the Salt Fork River. Right now he was heading for that same place.

He recalled what he had said then, "Tom, if I could get a section like this along a stream, with willows and cottonwoods for shade when the stock drinks, and grass enough to keep them strong, I wouldn't ask for more."

"I would too," Tom answered, "but it ain't for sale. Belongs to the government, I guess, if you look at that benchmark with the stamp on it. Besides, if it was, as penniless as I am, my rich aunt in Vermont would have to die first and leave me the money to buy it."

"I'm not joking, Tom. This place has most of the necessities for living. A fellow could make it self-sufficient in no time."

As he galloped along, Jim kept a sharp eye out for signs toward that place which he knew he was approaching. He had a location bump as some called it, but it could have been a highly developed sense of awareness, almost like an added sixth sense of direction. It was not long until Barney jumped over a creek bed as dry as a buffalo skull. Jim would like to have stopped for a look around but that was impossible. He had a haunting feeling that this was the streambed he had crossed nine years before. Sure enough, the silhouette of trees gradually came into view.

A tingle of elation raced through him, stimulating every cell in his body. Just to know he could depend on his memory to fulfill the dream of possessing even a quarter of that section was satisfaction enough. Jim looked behind him and veered straight toward those trees. He could see he was far enough ahead of the few riders behind, and by remembering the location of the old surveyor mound, he was confident that he could drive in his stake before anyone arrived to challenge him. Sure enough, the little pile of rocks surrounding the benchmark was intact enough that left no doubt in Jim's mind that he had found the right place. He pulled in the reins and made a short stop, like he was roping a doggie. In a split second he dismounted and grabbed the stake which had been secured to the thongs of the saddle with a slip knot, unsheathed his long knife, made a hole in the ground and drove in the stake which had a white banner with his name emblazoned on it.

The riders passing by at that time probably could not have heard Jim's words but they knew he meant business and passed on. Had they listened, they would have heard him declare, "This quarter section belongs to Jim Crouch and I claim it for myself, all one hundred and sixty acres." Then he found a stone nearby, pounded the stake securely and gave a loud shout, waving his arms while dancing a little jig around in homesteader's delight.

"Hurrah! Hurrah! Barney, you sure earned some oats for that wondrous ride. I'll sow a big patch of oats for you, but right now you will have to graze around in this dry grass scrounging for yourself." Jim forgot about the grain in his bedroll. He forgot to look at his watch. His elation was primal.

His thirst came first. After drinking from the canteen in gulps, he took off his old Stetson, poured some water in it and let Barney drink all he could spare, while thinking that this animal had resources of power to match his courage. After that he put the hobbles on Barney's forelegs, took off the bridle and saddle, gave him a slap on the rump and directed him toward the dry creek.

A flood of ideas swamped Jim's mind. He noticed that the grazing in these parts looked fairly promising even though the grass had dried out. Compared to the blue grass on Kentucky plantations it was lacking in beauty and moisture. He recalled his parents' land where he was born and had lived until he was 15, but that did not lessen his gratitude for his new homestead. The difference was that this was his.

The sod looked perfect for cutting up in ribbons with the sod plow he would bring in the covered wagon. It would make good sod bricks for the dugout they would have to live in at first, on account of the cyclones. He walked around the meadows in search of the pasture he planned to fence once he located and marked the corners of the four forty acres, which he would enclose one at a time. The new homesteader became so engrossed with the endless possibilities of his claim with its flat surface for the planting and harvesting of the wheat that he forgot to eat the lunch he brought. In the late afternoon he went looking for Barney. He knew he couldn't get far with the hobbles and suspected he would seek shade. Sure enough Jim found him under the cottonwoods where the willows began. Here in what otherwise was a dry creek bed, Barney had pawed a declivity in the sand and a trickle of water seeped to the surface.

"By Jimminy!" Jim cried as he knelt down, filled his cupped hands, and drank of the life giving water. "Sweet water, better than gold. Lucky day! What more can a man expect?"

His faithful horse got a petting and hand scratching under the chin signifying that he had done something deserving. "Good boy!" Jim said. "You've got a quarter section of your own to graze over tonight." Then he remembered. "In the morning you will get a treat of that grain Ott wanted you to have."

Several riders passed and looked longingly towards the newly staked claim. They rode on in search of unclaimed land. Then the first vehicles that Jim had seen passed some distance to the east. Up until then only men on horseback rode past Jim's claim. One looked like a wagon and another appeared to be a surrey gauging from that distance. Before long a stagecoach loaded with passengers and drawn by a span of black mules and another span of brown, passed close. The skinner on top and the passengers inside waved or nodded from the vehicle windows.

"For once in my life I'll bet I'm the envy of everybody passing here. Just hope they all keep going and none of them come in bothering me until I get my claim registered," Jim remarked to himself almost prayerfully. He watched from his wide-open vista. Few riders, after crossing the Salt Fork, rode west on the far side of the row of cottonwood trees. Throughout the remaining afternoon and on into the twilight the new homesteader watched the thinning stream of riders pass by. His emotions were mixed, and sometimes the sights were discouraging. In the distance he saw a spill and watched a lone rider pick himself up but failed to see the horse get back on his feet. Others passing by waved and shouted hilariously. Meanwhile Jim ate his jerky, prunes and hardtack, leaving a piece of rock candy for later. He was too excited to be hungry but he munched anyway, oblivious to what he was doing.

It had been a long day. There would never be another day quite the same for Jim, for the Territory, or for tens of thousands of people involved with the opening of the Cherokee Strip.

CHAPTER 3

CLAIM JUMPERS

Jim Crouch was not a pious man. Some would say he was irreligious. That would not be accurate for he had respect for every form of religion, but not for hypocrisy. His code of conduct encompassed the Golden Rule and until he made this race he could say that he had lived up to it. He pondered on his determination to beat his competitors, feeling a sense of guilt that he had taken every advantage of his skills and showmanship with Barney. He justified his actions as being inspired by his wife and family. He had never been faced with defending himself and wondered if he could kill a man, even though he had rubbed elbows with all kinds of outlaws. Jim did not like liquor, hated braggarts, and always had something else to do rather than frequent saloons and get mixed up in brawls. Nor was he a gambler, he even disliked cards, and was not a particularly good shot. His best way of survival was to attend to his own business, and that he did.

Jim was tired and the day had been exhausting, especially the long wait prior to the Race. The rest he needed included sleep, so he spread out the saddle blanket and put his bedroll on top of it, setting the corn and fodder aside on the dry grass. It felt good to stretch out and un-kink his legs. The sustained twilight faded into a starry sky. The first-quarter moon rose. Venus was flickering brightly in the west, while Jim's heavy eyelids fluttered shut, but not for long.

Suddenly Jim jerked up on his elbow. He was sure he heard Barney whinny. As he listened he peered out in the moonlit night. He had just been asleep long enough to become disoriented. Now he was sure he could see two objects moving in his direction. For an instant he wondered where he was, then suddenly he remembered that he might be called upon to defend his claim. The two objects appeared to be riders, not close yet, but advancing. Jim reached under his saddle, withdrew his only weapon, a Bowie knife, and left the sheath underneath. As a lad Jim had played mumblety-peg[1] with knives and had become an expert in handling and throwing knives. He was confident that he could handle one man in an emergency but with another one he would have to wait for developments.

"Howdy stranger. We're ridin' in," spoke a voice from the dark.

"Come on in if you're friendly, if not, stay away," Crouch shouted.

"What you doin' on my claim," a gravely voice threatened. "Don't you know that you cain't have my land? You take your gear and git goin'. This place is mine and we've got this carbine to prod you out of here." A rifle pointed toward Jim.

"You've never been on this land before," Jim barked. "It wasn't staked. My own stake is the only one near the benchmark. You fellows get your own homestead. This one is mine and I'm keeping it. No one beat me to it. I led the pack. You are either Sooners or claim jumpers. In either case the law is on my side."

"Law? What's law out here? Come on, git goin'," said the gravely voice. "Haven't you heard that possession is nine-tenths of the law and we're takin' possession. Git goin' before we git rough with you."

"Show me your permit," Jim demanded. "Bet you don't have one."

"Nobody's goin' to tell us what we've got to have. This gun is all we need." The moon allowed just enough light to see silhouettes. They were not quite sure what weapon Jim was holding so they hesitated. Jim knew that no sane man would start shooting in the dark. There were too many disadvantages and too easy a way to get killed.

"Did you hear me?" The gravely voice demanded again, making a pretense of lunging toward Jim. "I said to git your gear and git goin', unless you want to pay us fer our land. But I warn you, cowpoke, it won't be cheap."

---

1 Mumblety-peg is a boy's game in which a pocket knife must be tossed from a number of positions so that it always lands with the blade stuck in the ground, the loser having to draw a peg from the ground with his teeth.

It was evident now to Jim that the ruffians wanted money more than to take away his claim but he also knew that the few dollars he had with him would not satisfy their greed so he began to stall.

"What did you have in mind?" His tone became more conciliatory. "Why don't you two dismount, and if we're going to talk things over lets take our time. I'm tired and I guess you both are too." Jim rested on his haunches holding his knife beside his right leg. He acted cool and unflustered despite the lump in his throat causing his Adam's apple to bob up and down.

"Sorry I ain't got any coffee but I do have part of a plug of tobacco in my duck jacket hanging over there on that brush, if you'd like a chaw," Jim offered. "While you're at it, my pipe is in the other pocket if you will hand it to me. There's some matches there too. I prefer a pipe to chawing. You fellas can have what's left of the plug if you've got a knife to divide it. The Horseshoe brand is supposed to be lucky but more Star brand is sold, I hear."

The renegades took their share and Jim watched the second man put his small knife back in his pants pocket. The ruffian handed over Jim's pipe and bundle of matches, along with the Duke's mixture, which he twirled by the string.

While the culprits were softening up the hard tobacco in their mouths before they could do any talking, Jim, still stalling, pretended he could not get a draft going in his pipe. He lit several matches using his left thumbnail in order to still keep the knife in his right hand hidden. He casually tossed each lighted match at the sack of corn behind him hoping it would smolder and possibly catch fire.

The light exposed Jim's face but not his right hand. He kept thinking of ways he could divert their attention. One of the horses strayed farther afield while grazing and the second man went after it. The reins were let down, but even with their bridles on and the bit in their mouths the animals were able to crop off the tall dry grass which grew in bunches around Jim's campsite. Several minutes had passed after Jim started smoking when he became conscious of smoldering heat. He hoped the ruffians would not feel or smell it yet.

The gravely-voiced man took charge and shaking a finger at Jim exclaimed, "Stranger, now we're goin' to talk turkey! What you got in mind to pay us for this claim? You'll admit it's a choice location and worth quite a bit of dough or somethin' equal. Don't think you're goin' to git away with an offer under a hundred dollars."

"A hundred dollars!" Jim exclaimed. "You must be loco. You men are not sodbusters, you are downright fleecers, trying to do me out of my property. You can't get money out of a turnip for all I got is ten dollars. I'll tell you what! I'm a reasonable man, I'll give you nine dollars and I'll just keep the dollar left for registering my claim. Isn't that fair?"

"Hell, no," the gravely voiced man said. "You've got a horse somewhere around and this here saddle ought to be worth a double eagle to boot. I'll take the money, all but the dollar you need," he demanded as he kicked the saddle. Then he came forward menacing Jim with the carbine shouting for him to unbuckle his holster and throw it on the grass.

"You varmints, you just don't want to leave a feller anything, do you?" Jim said slowly, still stalling but finally throwing down his knife. At that instant several loud explosions shot white particles up into the air. The horses stampeded and ran in opposite directions.

"Don't stand there, you idiot!" the gravely voiced ruffian yelled at his partner. "Go after the horses before his dynamite goes off agin'. Let's git outta here. All hell's broke loose!" Then he took to his heels running after his own horse.

"Whew," Jim exclaimed out loud. "That's the second worst spot I ever got out of." He felt mighty grateful to Lizzie's old man and her brother Ott for that small gift of popcorn. "The wonder is that it worked. Really got me out of a pickle in the nick of time."

CHAPTER 4

THE CLAIM

If indeed the day of the Run to the Cherokee Strip was the most important day of his life, with the exception of the day he married the delightful Lizzie Bevis, then that night was equally memorable to Jim Crouch. He had raced from the Kansas border into the Outlet, galloping from noon to about 3:30 P.M. hardly slackening his speed to look back, or to wet his parched throat, until he drove in his stake and claimed the quarter section he wanted. Free government land was reserved for the swift. A prize of that size, a quarter mile square, was not offered every day. Jim felt elated that he was able to defend his claim even if he felt uneasy about a possible return of the bandits. One could never tell about such renegades.

Jim went back to his bedroll and slept from exhaustion and bone weariness. Nightmares plagued him. After a couple of hours of restless sleep, he heard Barney whinny three times, then heard a faint voice some distance away. The tone of distress grew louder and he distinctly heard someone calling for help. "Water!" Jim grabbed his canteen and mindful of the night's earlier events, cautiously moved out to meet the man who was limping towards him, and who now fell to his knees. "Water!" Jim pressed the container to the poor fellow's lips, telling him to take it easy. The man looked up to see his benefactor's face and recognized him in the moonlight.

"Why, Jim Crouch, it's you! Not all my luck has left me. That nag of mine stumbled in a foxhole and threw me, and at the same time broke her foreleg. She fell on my leg and about crushed my foot."

"Hank!" Jim exclaimed. "Well, that's pretty tough luck. Sorry what happened, but sure glad you found me. Let me help you to the campsite and I'll get some turpentine from my knapsack. I always carry some." He applied oil to the injured foot.

"The worst thing I ever had to do was to shoot the poor animal and go on foot." Hank said. "I threw my saddlebags over my shoulders and kept going. I walked until my ankle began to swell and then the boot had to come off. About the time I couldn't stand my weight on it anymore, I heard a horse whinny, figured someone was near, and I came your way."

"Yes," Jim replied. "It's hard to part with an animal, but it was all you could do. It's the risk we take in running a race like this one."

"Jim, take my bandanna to wrap my foot after you've finished," Hank requested. "Ouch! Do you have to be so rough? Think any bones are broken?"

"Hank, one thing I'm not is a doctor. Your foot is so swollen I couldn't tell anyway, but this I do know, that foot can't be walked on for days, maybe weeks."

"Jim, I haven't given up yet," Hank said emphatically. "I still want to locate a claim. You can help me, Jim. Loan me your horse for a few hours. I can see in the moonlight. Everything I ever wanted is tied up in this run. I just cain't give up. No siree, I cain't. I've come too far."

There was silence for several minutes while Jim walked to and fro in deep thought.

"Well, if I let you ride Barney to find a claim close by, I might be robbing my father-in-law of that chance. You see, he is an old Union soldier, who injured his leg in a battle. I told him I would try to help him get near where I'll be, so we could both use the same cyclone cellar[1]. There's not too much digging if we get a dugout done together to live in at first." Jim paced a few more minutes. "I'll tell you what I've worked out in my mind but I'm asking a favor in return. You will have to hand that Colt you're wearing over to me while you're gone. That won't be tonight but you can leave before dawn. You weren't the only visitor I had tonight. Two claim-jumpers tried to steal my claim. They were the worst kind of ruffians, and it was only a stroke of luck that I outwitted them and I don't think they took it too easily. They may return and I'll need to have that Colt to surprise them if they do." I don't have to tell you that if you don't find a claim in the first two hours you will have to return Barney to me for I'll let nothing stop me from registering my claim tomorrow."

---

1 Cyclone cellar, or storm cellar, is an underground shelter, in or adjacent to a home, and used as a refuge from severe storms.

"Jim," Hank said. "I'll be glad to part with the Colt. You kin keep the pistol if ya need it. All I want is a chance to git myself a homestead. I'll show ya how to raise wheat and I kin do dozens athings fer ya that'll be helpful if ya jist give me the chance to git some land. I'll show ya what gratitude is fer the rest of my life."

Hank unbuckled his holster and handed it over to Jim who walked over to the bedroll and put the weapon under the saddle.

After a few hours of much needed sleep, they woke up as dawn broke quietly and tones of cerise and purple colored the sky. Jim saddled Barney who was grazing nearby, helped Hank mount and wished him good luck as he rode away. Within a few minutes the sky was ablaze and the sparse clouds looked like coals of fire, which reminded him that he was hungry and he had nothing to cook even if that planetary fireplace was available for him to use. Jim noted a bush of sand plums nearby still left with some fruit drying on the limbs. He was glad to see the wild plums on his lands, especially since Lizzie made clear tart jelly from them. But right now he had cottontails on his mind so he lost no time in seeking his game. He did not have to go far. They came out from their night cover disturbed by Jim's movement. He fired at the first cottontail, missed, but shot a larger rabbit as it scurried away. With some dried cow chips, and a few branches of dried limbs from the willows and a fat little bunny, he had the makings of a fine meal. In minutes Jim skinned and gutted the carcass. It was like old times on the lone prairie with nature's survival kit.

The rabbit was young and quickly dressed. Without either frying pan or grease, Jim decided he would make a mudpack and cook this special treat in the coals of the fire. He searched Hank's saddlebags and sure enough, he found salt folded in slick butcher paper. He smeared the inside of the rabbit with salt. Then he hustled round for some dry sage and mustard while he was looking for more cow chips to build up the fire. The Arbuckle coffee and can to brew it in was the best find yet.

Jim couldn't help reminiscing about his early days. His cooking skill went back to the Kentucky plantation where Martha, one of their black servants, had been the cook. Following his mother's death when he was no more than six years old, Martha did what she could to console the little boy. The Crouches had freed their slaves, hoping to avoid civil strife when the threat of war between the states loomed on the horizon. Ossie and Martha were the only slaves who refused their freedom. Martha saw with foresight that one of the four Crouch sons would need to cook, so she started with Jim. Having him near her in this shared activity did much to ease his grief. The kindly black woman shared her wisdom and patience with the boy, and he would always remember her with gratitude and affection for her help during that sad time. Neither Jim nor Martha ever dreamed that he would end up cooking for a cattle outfit, which he had been forced to do a few years back, not far from where he now stood. Much had transpired since then, but he still held on to the memory.

He was riding as a wrangler for a large cattle outfit during those years when he first learned to know the Cherokee Strip. Jim had been sent out to one of the far sections after some strays. On his return to camp three days later, bone weary and hungry as a bear, he sauntered down to the cook shack expecting a square meal to be served up pronto by Quinn, the current Irish cook. Instead, he found Quinn wall-eyed drunk, and writhing in pain for having connected with a nest of wasps. Enterprising as Jim was, he wasted no time in fixing his own meal. From the butcher's rack he took down a well-hung hind-quarter of beef, cut off a good-sized slab of meat and pounded the hell out of it to make it tender. From the coal scuttle next to the stove he ignored the large chunks and picked out small hunks and some coal dust to quickly heat up the stove. In no time the stove was ready and he put the biscuits he had made in the oven, heated some beans, fried his meat and made coffee from some ground Lion Head coffee beans. With a sigh of satisfaction, he sat and chomped on the steak. At that point company entered the back door. Dave Larson, the range boss, and Tom Miller, one of Jim's old sidekicks, walked in.

Jim swallowed a few more choice morsels before he said a word. Between mouthfuls he greeted them, "Sit down and drink a cuppa coffee with me. Just help yourselves. You know where the mugs are. What are you sidewinders up to now? Don't tell me though if there's any bad news. Want to enjoy my own cooking first."

"All right," Larson said. "Your report can wait unless you've found something that needs attention."

"Nope," replied Jim. "Only that I found evidence that some rustlers had a camp 'bout two miles from that old line shack near the border of the Darlington lease. Musta bin three or four days before. I knew they were long gone. Why don't you bronco busters have a biscuit?" Jim offered as he passed the pan around. "Help yourself to the butter and sorghum[2]. You're not as tired as I am you can get a plate over there." He pointed to a stack on the open rack.

"Say Jim, you old deceiver," remarked Miller. "Here you had me thinkin' that you couldn't do anything but rope and ride and skin buffalo. Where'd you ever learn to cook like this? Why these biscuits are light as thistledown. I thought I knew all your tricks, but in all the time I knowed you, I never once dreamed you could cook. I'm flabbergasted!"

Jim had rather enjoyed his command of the kitchen but he never suspected that he would lose his hard-earned spurs on account of it. At that moment Jim did not know that Quinn had been threatening to quit for some time. The cook had been on two or three tears in the last month, as if asking to get fired. The cowhands were dissatisfied. Chow was next in importance to their wages. Larson had been in a quandary as to what to do about it until he had entered the cook shack.

A few minutes later Larson pushed his chair back. Tom got up too. Only Jim, who had not finished, remained at the table.

"Jim, never mind your report," said Larson sternly, "I've decided that you cain't ride for this outfit no more. You're fired! Take off them spurs, you've got to trade them for an apron. But you'll make more money cookin' for the outfit than ridin' for it. Instead of thirty dollars a month and found, I'll raise your wages to thirty-five. Just make out your list of supplies, and I'll git 'em."

Jim didn't like to lose his independence, but he was a practical person. After some thought he answered, "Tell you what, Larson, I'll help you out of your predicament for sixty days, but no more than that. I didn't hire out to cook. I'm a cowhand. Two months

---

2 Sorghum, though sometimes called molasses was made from the sweet juicy stalks of cereal grains.

will be long enough to be out of my saddle. That'll be long enough for you to find another cook, and you'd better get one."

Jim stirred himself from thinking about old times, and returned to the present, gazing at his claim. He looked to his right, where he saw all kinds of rigs passing by in the distance, one by one, still pursuing free government land. Then he saw a rider approaching from the left. He recognized Barney's whinny and he put the coffee into the boiling water. Hank had been gone for more than two hours.

"Hi ho Jim!" Hank called out victoriously. "Staked my claim right next to yours, found the surveyor's peg among some brush and dry weeds where it musta bin overlooked by the fast riders in the twilight hours. Gosh, that coffee smells great. Help me down and we'll have a cupful to celebrate. What else is cookin'? I smell somethin' mighty fancy, like prairie hens 'r somethin'."

Jim helped Hank down from Barney. "If you staked your claim so close to mine, what took you so long, Hank?" Jim asked him.

"Well, Jim," Hank answered. "It took quite a spell to find the bench mark which, as I said, was covered with brush an' rock. When I tried to drive in my stake the ground was like hardpan, so hard that I broke my knife handle. I had a deuce of a time sinkin' that stake deep enough to hold it fast. Then I gathered up rocks and made a mound like yours Jim. Of course I wanted to follow the dry creek bed a little bit, both ways, to get the lay of the land. I think it's going to be first rate. But let me tell you about the sight I seen that only one man in a million would have a chance to see."

"What's that? Come on Hank!" Jim exclaimed. "Only one in ten million has a chance to register a free hundred and sixty acre claim today and here I am waiting and listening to you when I ought to be long on my way to Alva to the land office." Jim motioned to him to help himself to the food, but Hank kept on talking excitedly.

"There was still some dew on the sage as Barney cantered along. Gad what a gait that critter has, like ridin' on air! Then there was a streak of rose in the east. I felt a slight breeze to my back and our scent carried ahead of us when suddenly wild animals started jumpin' up all around us. I saw antelope an' coyotes, jack rabbits an' cottontails crossing our path and Barney never shyin' at any of 'em. It was then I concluded what was happenin'. I guess the thousands of hoof beats in the race had scared these animals outta their natural shelters and they were in a race for survival theirselves. They'd bin chased this way to the sidelines until Barney and me scared 'em up again. The little critters were there too, skunks and 'possum with no trees to climb. Honest, Jim, I'm not exaggeratin'. The funny thing I thought was, Run you critters while you're free, for it won't be long until us homesteaders will be on your trail. And that's it. What's more Jim, I never before felt so free myself."

Jim had helped Hank to alight, as he shared his strange experience. Full of curiosity, Jim said, "I wondered what that rumbling noise was. I was also concerned about how you would manage to get back up on Barney again. But to answer your question about what's cooking, I scared up a young cottontail just as you left. Reason it smells so different, I grabbed a handful of dry mustard and sage and filled its innards with the crumbled dry leaves. Takes away the wild taste."

"Well Jim, I had a little luck," Hank said. "When I was ready to leave there, Barney stood still and let me take my time gettin' the foot in the stirrup, like he knew what was goin' on. I swung my chest up in the saddle afore I raised up the rest of my body like ya do when you're mountin' for a bareback ride. That there hoss surely has a good head on his shoulders," Hank explained gratefully.

"What worries me, Hank," Jim said, "is how you're going to get to the County Seat to file your claim. Want me to buy you another nag while I'm in Alva filing my claim? I can't lose much more time, if I can help it."

"Jim, I got to make a sorry confession," Hank said."I'm almost dead broke, can't buy another nag. Just got my filing fee and a bit of small change to buy a few groceries. Course, I could sell ya the Colt, but ya probably don't need a pistol anymore. Could I ride double with ya if that ain't too much to ask?"

"Let's get that rabbit cooled off so we can eat." Jim held the coffee can with his bandanna and poured the rich brew into each tin cup. They clinked the cups to signify a tremendous achievement.

It took them only a few minutes to consume the wild game and to finish their coffee. Although his breakfast had put him in a better frame of mind, all Jim could think of was getting to the Land Office in Alva to file and register his government claim.

"Come on, Hank," Jim said, as soon as they had finished eating, "let's not lose another minute. Let me boost you up behind me for the start. Gosh-almighty! Almost forgot to tromp out the fire." In another minute Jim swung his leg over the saddle and thrust his feet into the stirrups. "The sun was high and Jim started Barney off at a brisk pace heading for Alva.

"Jim, have you ever done any real farmin'," Hank asked, "like samplin' the best soil you've got suitable fer growin' wheat? If ya don't know that fer a start, your crop could fail, seed and labor wasted. Know-how is what I've got and I'm goin' to give ya all I have. Ya can't appreciate what know-how means when it comes to farmin'. Jim, you've done me the greatest favor any man can do fer another. I'm goin' to make ya glad ya did me this exceptional favor, if it takes me a lifetime to prove it."

"I expect there's plenty I don't know," Jim answered, "me never caring for anything much besides stock, and having a fair eye for horse-flesh. It's kinda comforting to start farming with a neighbor that knows what he's doing. All I really know was what I learned working on my Pa's Kentucky plantation when I was a little tike, and that's what made me decide to be a roaming cowpoke. I recall one year we had a pest of locusts. They ate the corn we planted, and cutworm got the potatoes before we did."

Hank leaned back and nearly fell off. "Whoa, Barney." Jim grabbed the reins to steady him.

"My mother, Mary Samuel Keene, was a fine horsewoman," Jim said. "Her family, the Samuel Keenes, raised thoroughbreds at their stable near Lexington, Kentucky. So I came naturally to fancy horseflesh. My paternal grandfather, Josiah Crouch, first had a plantation near Jonesboro, Tennessee. They raised thoroughbreds also. Grandpa had five brothers, and when the plantation there got too crowded, he moved to Kentucky."

Barney maintained a steady pace. Jim went on. "My brother Keene and his friend Charlie and I rode all the way from Louisville, Kentucky to Missouri on horseback seeking riding fame. I was a boy of fifteen when we started, but ended up a man in Kansas about a year later. Once, on our way, we were mistaken for some road agents that a posse was seeking all the way from Montana. They looked us over and seeing that I wasn't the bearded bandit one description called for since I only had a few hairs on each side of my upper lip, they let us go on our way." Jim paused, "Sorry, I didn't mean to get off the subject of farming. Bet you could show me plenty."

"Yep, farmin' is all I know." Hank said. "It's all I ever done. I worked for Pa since I was a little shaver but he never paid me no wages. Just gave me a pig at Christmas time or somethin' like that. One Christmas when I was still in knickers Pa gave me that sorrel nag. She was like one a' the family. Sure was tough to have to shoot her yesterday. Hate like the dickens to have to write the sorry news to the folks and about my bum foot too. But if I get my claim registered, that will be good enough news to soften the bad. Got to git that letter off today. Howie, my younger brother, will have to bring Ellie, my wife, when he brings the supplies in the covered wagon. I'm afraid I'm goin' to be a nuisance until they get here. Pa will put up the money fer the seed wheat and I'll pay him back after I sell the first crop. I'm willin' to pay you back with interest anything that you do for me until then, Jim."

"Aw shucks, Hank! Stop telling yourself you're in the way. It's a fine thing to know we can work together at planting and when we reap the harvest. Besides, your wife and Lizzie can keep each other company, especially since we're going to have an addition in February," Jim announced proudly.

"Now ain't that a co-in-ci-dence? Ellie is in the family way too, and expectin' about the same time. With no midwives in sight, they might have to depend on each other for the bornin'," said Hank in his practical way.

Jim dismounted Barney to lighten the load. The men gazed at the monotonously level landscape from horizon to horizon. The only difference in appearance between this area and the Crouch and Hartner claims was that they were riding now through a growth of fresh green prairie grass. It was evident that there had been rain here earlier.

After a spell, Jim mounted Barney again. "Do you find this territory to your liking, coming from Iowa?" Jim asked.

"What do you mean, Jim? If plowin' a straight furrow is what you mean, yes. Looks all alike here, but there certainly wasn't any rain over our way, or it would be green there too."

"That's what I mean," Jim answered, "It can rain cats and dogs in one place and on the other side of the acre, not a drop will fall. The Outlet is like that, rain squalls."

"I see what you mean. In Ioway we have more general rains where most of the state gets drenched," Hank explained. "It's colder too. Sometimes the winter gets so cold that a neighbor of ours put out a bucket of boilin' water on the porch to see how long it would take to freeze. It froze so fast that the ice was still hot. Then the summers are so all fired hot sometimes that this same neighbor told me he had seen a coyote chasin' a rabbit, and they wuz both walkin'."

"Hank," Jim laughed, "you'd better save those stories for our first hoedown!"

After a while he asked, "How are you riding back there? Whoa Barney." Jim jumped down again. "My legs need stretching, guess I'll walk for a little now." Barney automatically adjusted to Jim's walking speed as Hank slipped forward into the saddle. The trail was level and the terrain stretched flat in all directions, except where prairie dog towns and mole-hills were scattered among the sage and buffalo grass. Everything in this section was bursting out green from an earlier downpour.

As he walked beside Barney, Jim said, "I'll swear nary a squall hit our claims. I've noticed this before in the Panhandle. Another difference you'll notice about this climate is the winds. Nothing to stop them, there are no big trees, no hills of any size. It blows sand and dirt, and doesn't know when to stop. Yep, you can not get away from it. We've got the gol-darned wind to contend with. Expect it and you won't be disappointed."

Late in the afternoon after each man had taken turns changing in the saddle, Jim was riding behind the cantle again when Hank asked, "Do you think we'll make the Land Office before they're closed for the night?"

"If I know the disposition of those Boomers they'll have to keep open until midnight or even later if there's a lineup to get registered," Jim answered wearily. The physical strain and the excitement of the previous twenty-four hours took a toll on even these two strong young men. Barney doggedly plodded on. The clinking of the bridle and the creaking of the leather were the only sounds on the rolling sea of prairie. Jim was too tired to wonder about his claim.

CHAPTER 5

THE LAND OFFICE

Late in the afternoon, Jim and Hank entered the dusty lane that led up to the Land Office in Alva. Seven miles had seemed more like seventy, and Barney showed the strain of his double burden. A long line of homesteaders waited to get inside to register their claims.

"You stay in the saddle Hank 'til my turn comes, then I'll let you go ahead of me," Jim said.

"Since you're my doctor, I'll obey!" Hank answered.

Jim felt the tension in the atmosphere. He looked at the town being born but he had not anticipated the drama of it. Down the lane, a crowd of riders milled about waiting for an auction of some town lots while the auctioneer took some time out. Other members of the crowd conferred with men still on horseback, as if giving them instructions. Among a motley gathering of hard-looking characters, Jim saw the two renegades who had tried to jump his claim the previous night. He hoped they wouldn't recognize him from their night-time encounter and he quickly turned away from them. At times like this he was glad he had no striking features to make him memorable.

Hank and Jim had been in line for what secmed like hours when Jim's turn came. Barney seemed content despite the milling confusion about him. Instead of going in to register his own claim, Jim helped Hank dismount and pushed him inside in his place so that Hank could register his claim. After about five minutes, Hank returned limping and waving his white paper. Jim then went in to register. He handed over his permit and fee to the government clerk who read the number of the surveyor's marker and entered the information in the record. The clerk then gave Jim his receipt. The quarter section was now registered and he proudly signed his name on the pages.

"Hey fellers!" Jim exclaimed, "Look, see this receipt? Now I'm the legal owner of a hundred and sixty acres of prairie land and I'd like to see the color of the man's eyes who thinks that he could take it away from me!" He drew breath and continued, "Neither brigand nor claim jumper had better try it either! Right Hank? And we got a Colt to back us up." He wanted to give notice to the two claim jumpers who were still in view.

Just then a familiar figure rode up to the hitching post outside the Land Office. His fringed buckskin jacket was still split down the back seam and his grizzled face matched the buckskin cayuse from which he dismounted.

"Hey there, Jim," Josh hollered at Jim. Then he saw Hank with his bandaged foot.

"Well, looky here, the three of us meet agin," Josh continued. "Didn't I tell ya about luck? Why Hank, did you get tromped in the rush?" Josh strode forward and shook Jim's hand and then grabbed Hank's hand with the other.

"If you're referrin' to my bandaged foot, yes." Hank answered. "I had the bad luck to lose my nag. She gave quite a spill and broke her leg. Had to shoot her before I reached the promised land. But as you see, a certain luck stuck with me and I found Crouch here," pointing to Jim, "which is the best luck yet, or I wouldn't be here wavin' this white paper."

"Josh, old timer, how 'bout you?" Jim asked. "Did you get your claim staked?"

"Yep, but it's only eighty acres," Josh replied. "I'm practically a city man, livin' just a couple a miles out of town. I was held back by a spill, myself. I got dumped when a slicker drivin' a livery stable rig sideswiped me and throwed me down. My head struck another rig, but I got up and grabbed the tailgate of another spring wagon as it swished by, 'til I saw my cayuse straight ahead. Then I took one leap into the saddle and kept agoin'. Come on out and I'll show you my diggins', boys."

"Can't, Josh," Jim answered. "Got to be on my way back to Pratt to bring in the supply wagon and bring back the missus and my little boy, Robbie. By the way, could you take care of Hank for a few days? He's low on funds and without a mount. Could he bunk with you? We rode double on Barney. But you could walk if you're a mind to for that short distance. Just as long as Hank stays off his leg."

"Fraid I'm goin' to be a nuisance," complained Hank.

"Don't you believe it!" Josh replied. "It's mighty lonesome out there if you don't mind bein' crowded. Just look at that sky. Looks like a real storm is brewin' up, don't it? Jim, if you're goin' to ride to the Kansas line tonight, you'd better be on your way. I'll look after Hank."

Jim saw the gathering clouds as he headed north, but he wanted to get on the road for Kansas. His family would worry until they knew that he was safe. He was certain that stories of the race and the injuries sustained by many claimants would precede him. He did not want to prolong the uncertainty for them, particularly for Lizzie.

He had not ridden more than a few miles when he ran into a thunder and lightning storm with the rain coming in slanting sheets of water. He wanted to stop but could find no shelter until he saw a clump of what turned out to be thorny sand plum bushes. As he approached, he saw what looked like one or two men, so he reined Barney back to the main trail again. Something was not right and he wanted no truck with any trouble tonight. Strange things could happen on a lonely road. So he kept on for another few miles, picking his way through the mud. His yellow slicker and hat did not keep him entirely dry although they kept him warm inside.

The muddy road and the noise of the storm seemed endless as Jim reached the Kansas line. This time he reached a large cluster of trees where Barney and he were able to take cover. Jim dismounted and loosened the cinches. He picked several handfuls of grass and brushed some of the water off the patient horse. A tired animal, warm as he was, would easily sicken if left rain-soaked and began to shiver. They waited a couple of hours until the storm abated and resumed the hard ride on into the night.

Back in Alva as soon as Jim rode off, Josh took Hank in tow and helped him into the nearby tent saloon. "You kin wait here while I go buy some grub," said Josh, as he stepped up to the bar. When the bartender saw the money in his customer's hand he shoved a bottle of whiskey and a glass jigger in front of Josh.

"Six bits a shot today," the bartender said. "Maybe a week from now we can charge less!"

A group down at the end of the bar caught Josh's interest. Loud talk came from half a dozen or so youngish men who had evidently made the Race and were trying to tell their experiences. They could not be heard over the din of the portable tin piano. One braggart among them threw down a twenty-dollar gold eagle and offered drinks to the others. The bartender said he could not make change for it.

"It's your hard luck," the braggart said, "it's the smallest I've got." Just then he turned around long enough for Josh to recognize Sharkey, the man he'd been looking for a long time.

Josh left the counter immediately and took a drink over to Hank.

"Stay here awhile, Hank. I got to buy some grub afore the storm breaks." The thunder and lightning exploded. Raindrops beat a staccato tattoo on the canvas roof of the improvised saloon, frightening some of the customers who left, Sharkey among them.

A half hour later Josh returned.

"Hank, come outside quick!" Josh called. Hank limped through the canvas flap. Outside, the rain came down in slanting sheets. Between the saloon and the next tent, Josh pointed to a man's form lying prone in the mud.

"Guess I'd better go for the marshal. Will you stay here, Hank? Lean on that pole."

During Josh's absence a stranger rode up on a sleek bay gelding. He wore a black slicker and rain hat. "Stand back!" he said. "This feller is a friend of mine and I'll take him over." He reached into the man's blood stained jacket pockets.

"It's just as I feared," said the stranger. "Someone tried to murder him for his gold pieces. That's what can happen to a feller when he drinks too much and his tongue loosens up!"

The stranger then commanded Hank to help carry him, which Hank was hard pressed to do. They placed the injured man behind the saddle. The man mounted, adjusted the heavy form over the horse's rump, spurred the bay and galloped off.

Hank, nonplussed by the speed with which the incident had occurred, had forgotten he was half crippled himself, and had failed to protest or ask questions. Without comment he had watched the stranger remove his rain soaked bandanna and thrust it into the bleeding chest wound of his luckless friend. Hank knew without a doubt it was not a bullet wound. A knife had done the damage. Anyone who had ever butchered a pig would know a large blade had done it.

Josh returned and was surprised to discover the disappearance of the wounded man. In a way he looked relieved.

"I couldn't find no marshal nor lawman of any kind, so it's just as well we didn't get mixed up in things that don't concern us."

The rain stopped abruptly but the skies were still threatening.

"We'd better git goin'." Josh continued. "I'll help you mount, if you'll hold this sack of flour with one hand, and the grub with the other."

Josh's cayuse was hard put to carry a double load, with his hooves sloshing and sliding in the mud. Finally, after the two-mile ride on a narrow straight path, Josh slid down from the buckskin and lifted Hank down, exclaiming, "Welcome to my humble lean-to!"

Hank hobbled as fast as he could, following Josh through the open door, almost stumbling over a broken crate. Josh struck a match and they could see somewhat around them.

"Why man," Hank exclaimed looking around, "you've done a pretty job of making a shelter so fast. This is real cozy like. You certainly lost no time gittin' set up."

"Things were movin' awful fast this mornin'. The train took two hours to unload. It brought everything from lumber to lard, from bushels of groceries to grain, tents and tarps, and even a tin piano and a car of livestock. I followed the dray that hauled the lumber. That's where I got the poles and crates to build this shelter. And of course the nails and the tarpaulin for the roof, and a good thing too or we would be as wet as a scalded chicken. Once in a while I guess I do things right," Josh said proudly. "Hank, you gettin' hungry? Let's have some cheese and crackers and maybe a can of sardines and some dried apples."

"Fraid I ain't very hungry now," Hank remarked, "my insides are still stirred up. Let's wait a spell to eat. I ain't never seen a man wounded to death before. I come from a most peaceful part of the country."

Later, after the cold supper, Hank remarked, "It's a good thing I wrote that letter to my wife, and got it off before the train pulled out. Did it while you were stockin' up grub in that grocery tent. Told them 'bout my hurt foot that's healin' fast, but that it might set me back some in diggin' the dugout. They'll know everything needed. Told her to bring Howie, my kid brother, to drive the team and supplies that was on the list I left at home. Pa can't read or write but I said to tell him I would pay him back when my first crop was harvested. Hope he won't be too disappointed that I'm not goin' back. I'm sure 'debted to you and Crouch. When you think of the broke condition I'm in! I'll never forgit it to my last day! Guess my best asset is my Colt revolver."

"Don't mention it, Hank, you'd do the same fer us. Besides you're a lot of company. I'm gittin' sleepy, how about you?" Josh added. "Guess we'll find some dry spots on the straw where we kin put our bedrolls, if you've got one with your saddlebags. If not, there's a little piece of tarp you kin use, which reminds me that Jim must be out there somewhere in the rain near the Kansas line by now, if this rain reaches that far. On second thought it'd be a waste of time to be concerned about Jim Crouch. He's one man that makes you certain that he kin take care of hisself. If I'm any judge he'll git everythin' he goes after fer I'm downright positive he's got that special thing that we call LUCK."

CHAPTER 6

LIZZIE'S JOURNEY

Mid-morning of September 16, Lizzie was resting in the shade of Pa Bevis's buckboard which was parked in a campground back from the Kansas border starting line. It was exceptionally warm and Lizzie was feeling queasy after cooking side meat and biscuits for breakfast for Jim, Pa Bevis and Ott. Right after eating Jim saddled Barney, tied on his saddlebags and bedroll, kissed Lizzie, and took off to find a good place in the crowded line to start his run.

Not one to sit idle, Lizzie opened the sewing bag she had brought with her and as she mended she thought back on the last two weeks in Pratt before they came here.

Jim had told her he knew the way to the claim he wanted from his wrangling days in the Outlet and he was determined to get there before anyone else. Pa Bevis put new shoes on Barney and Jim made sure Barney was in top running shape for this most important race. They would leave Pratt three days before the big race so they could travel easily and not tire Barney.

While the men planned the race, Lizzie fretted over what goods to pack in their covered wagon for their move to the claim, and what to leave behind for Pa Bevis to bring later. She knew she would have to bring as much as possible with her as they would be living out of the wagon for some time. She was thankful they'd been able to save enough money to buy seed for their first planting along with a little extra for emergencies.

She was startled out of her reverie when she heard her name called out. Looking up from her sewing she recognized the Farrells from Chillicote way walking towards her. What a surprise, she thought, to see people she knew from home here at the race. They stopped to talk for a few minutes, explaining they were looking for their son and his wife who were hoping to get some property in the new town of Alva. Lizzie wished them luck in their quest as they hurried away, saying they hoped they would see her again later.

"Ott, take this corn and tobacco to Jim, and don't forget the grub Lizzie fixed for him," Pa said when he came back from taking care of their team. "He was too pesky to listen to anything this morning. Maybe you can persuade him to take the things now."

"The troopers seem to be having a hard time keeping the folks back," Lizzie said to Pa. "No matter what they do, they can't stretch the whole length of the line, can they? I'll bet some Sooners have got through anyway. Hope none of them gets to Jim's claim."

"The sun has been up for ages, it MUST be noon," Lizzie said to her father. "I want to see them go, but I'm so hot I feel nauseated. I don't want to leave the buckboard. I wonder if I could lie down a spell. Oh oh, something seems to be happening. The horses are acting up, poor brutes. So many of them have been standing in line since dawn. The heat, the flies, the dust!"

Lizzie climbed into the front of the buckboard and stood up just as the shots rang out and the waiting throng took off. She thought she saw Jim and Barney out in front before the dust covered the racing homesteaders. She was dismayed to see a young woman fall out of a buggy when her husband turned the rig sharply. The dust became a thick cloud covering the whole area. Lizzie turned away from the frenzied rush, not wanting to see any more accidents. Sitting down on the buckboard seat, she said a little prayer for Jim's safekeeping.

Later, when Pa turned them for home she lay down in the back with Robbie, his head on the carpetbag. They expected to make two stops going home, one at Thatcher's and another at Jim's folks, with hopes it wouldn't put them out too much. Before falling asleep herself Lizzie looked at Robbie nestled beside her. He's been a pesky little varmint ever since we came on this trip, she thought, but I wanted him to be here for his Pa even though he's really too young to remember any of it.

When Jim got the claim they would have a settled home at last. Before Lizzie met Jim she was weary of traveling. The Bevis family had been to so many places since Pa took the family out of Indiana. He would buy and sell horses everywhere they went, and Lizzie would help him and Ma. They'd be glad to see a month with a couple of dollars to spare. But for all that, they had much to thank the Good Lord for. Pa had always done right well for his family. They never did see a day when they didn't have enough. Every month Pa and Ma managed to put a little bit by against the day when they could get a place of their own. Lizzie hoped Pa would manage to get a claim close to Jim's so her Ma could help her deliver. She had helped with the birthing of her Ma's younger ones and was glad to be able to do it. A woman needed such skills in these parts.

That was how Lizzie met Jim. She was helping with the birthing of the Crouch twins, when both the Bevis and Crouch families were neighbors in Pratt, before the Crouches moved to Medicine Lodge. Jim came to his Pa and his step-mother to bring fresh cow's milk. Lizzie had seen many men in different places. But she knew when she saw him that he was the man for her. He stood so tall and straight, and he spoke so plain. As she got to know him better, she could see the strength of purpose in everything he did. A strong, honest man wasn't easy to find. Sure, there were four or five men to every woman, but not the kind a woman wanted to settle down with. She had noticed that the men who moved west were either running away from something they had done, or were still searching, always on the move. A strong man with a sense of determination didn't happen too often. Now after two years, Lizzie felt the marriage was better than ever.

When we get the claim I'll be glad to work by his side to make a real homestead, Lizzie said to herself. We'll have to work harder than our parents ever did. But isn't that what building the frontier means? Our children will never have to have it as hard as we did. At least we can give them that. We can point the right way, and leave the rest to the Lord. I'm excited, but I'm weary too.

They left the line about 3:30 p.m. and going at about seven miles an hour, they expected to arrive at Gerlane, eighteen miles from the Line in time to eat supper there with the Thatchers. If all went well they could still get to Jim's folks later at Medicine Lodge, another seven miles from Gerlane.

Robbie woke up again. Lizzie gave him a little cornbread and some apple juice, and he crawled forward to ride up front between Pa and Ott. She lay down to rest for a while.

***

Mrs. Thatcher and Josie, her youngest girl, made them right welcome. Josie took Robbie to see the puppies while Mrs. Thatcher and Lizzie caught up on their news and finished cooking the supper. Young Seth was the only man left at home. The rest of the family was down on the Line too. They were in Kiowa, east of where Lizzie and Pa Bevis had been. They were still down there partying along with other neighbors.

Brother Ott was glad to visit with Seth. He untied the pony behind the wagon, and the boys helped Pa Bevis unhitch the buckboard, feed and water the team and let the horses roll in the corral to shake off the dirt and sweat from the last twenty-four hours. At leaving time they gave them a good rub-down before the men put the tackle on again and hitched the team to the buckboard.

Mrs. Thatcher showed Lizzie her new things from the Montgomery Ward catalog. She was an order taker for several of her neighbors and herself thereby saving on the shipping charges. Montgomery Ward dispatched the orders, the Thatchers collected the goods from the railroad station, and their neighbors came by to get their goods. Lizzie thought it a good idea. Everyone saved a little and it seemed right neighborly. She hoped she could do that in Oklahoma Territory if they were near a depot.

Besides being excited with the notion of homesteading, Lizzie felt a bit scared. Poor Jim, she thought. He always says I never get flustered, and that I'm always so calm. If only he knew, it's another big change for me. I'm four months along now and we'll be a ways from anywhere. I wonder if there'll be any neighbor women close by. I'd hate to have to trouble Jim at a time like that, but of course we'll do whatever we must, since my time is still five months away.

Mrs. Thatcher gave them a good supper: fried chicken, okra, black-eyed peas and buttered biscuits, fresh peach pie, cream, lots of good coffee, and milk for young Robbie. Her guests were so grateful. She seemed pleased to get the crocheted chair-backs Lizzie had promised her last Easter when they were all together visiting the Crouches at Medicine Lodge.

They were on their way again about eight. Lizzie and Robbie bedded down in back. Ott was still racing and shouting at Seth as they left. He spelled Pa with the driving. A couple of miles beyond Gerlane it poured rain and they took shelter in some cottonwoods that gave hardly any cover from the storm. They got going again in a couple hours. Robbie woke up cross as two sticks. He kept getting out from under the blanket and Lizzie could not keep him dry. He whined all the way to Medicine Lodge.

They pulled in after midnight. She was so tired she was even glad to see Ma Crouch, who was surprisingly kind to her this time and brought hot water, a nice clean towel, and then put her to bed with some hot tea. She hardly recalled sinking into that soft, clean bed. It felt mighty good after all that time in the buckboard. The night before at the Line she was long awake listening to Jim go over his plans. Ma Crouch put Robbie in the crib in her room, but he was in Lizzie's bed at first light.

Fall was one of the loveliest times and everything smelled so good after the rain even if it was a hot Indian summer. The travelers were up about 6:30, late because of the long haul the previous day. Ott had already looked after the stock. They left after breakfast around 9 a.m. and still had twenty-eight miles to Pratt.

Pa had shared their experiences with the Crouches the night before, and Lizzie talked with Ma Crouch in the morning. They discussed the plan for Pa Bevis to go back down again to the claim after Jim and Lizzie left Pratt. Lizzie felt sure Jim did get the claim.

Lizzie wondered if her sister Vena made the Race, and if she did, how she went, and where did she start. She hoped Pa would forgive Vena's defiance. It made Ma feel so sad to lose track of her. She wondered too, if Jim's brother Keene and his friend went from Kiowa. It would be days before they'd find out.

They stopped to eat the midday meal four miles south of Sawyer, leaving maybe fifteen miles to Pratt. They pulled off the road and unpacked the basket Ma Crouch had given them filled with buttermilk, cold meat, cornbread, oatmeal cookies and half a watermelon. The meal tasted so much better just to rest and eat. Pa took it easy on the team so they went a little slower than earlier in the journey. Robbie saw some places he recognized and felt calmer, though he still wriggled about like an eel. Pa helped him hold the reins now and then to let him think he was doing the driving, which made Robbie feel good. Ott helped her too. He took Robbie on his knees and told him how he helped Jim pack in the corn and tobacco in the saddlebags, and how at the Line Barney was chomping at the bit and stomping, and about all the people waiting for the shot to signal the start of the Race at noon. Lizzie worked on a piece of her crochet as she was too worn out to do anything else. She went over the packing lists in her head again, not wanting to forget anything important.

Pa stopped at the general store beyond Sawyer to ask of any news of the Race. Other travelers had relayed stories of people injured in accidents, and collisions and capsized rigs and wagons. They said there were crowds at all the Land Offices later on the day of the Race. The rumors weren't of anyone they knew.

They stopped again where a creek crossed the road beyond Sawyer. They drank water, had a piece of jerky, finished the cookies, and refilled the water jug. The team drank and cooled their hooves at the edge of the stream. It felt good to stretch their legs. When they finally got home they shared the news and experiences of the last few days. Jim was on their minds and Ma joined hands with them all for a short prayer. They asked a blessing for his safe return, and offered thanks for their own safe journey. Lizzie offered her gratitude for the animals that had taken them there and back, over a hundred miles in five days.

The next day Lizzie got up early, unpacked the large carpetbag and did the laundry. She hemmed several of the clean flour sacks and sewed them together to make two crib sheets. She hung the rest of the sacks in the sun for a few hours before putting them away for later use as clothing or household articles.

Several neighbor ladies came over in the afternoon for a quilting bee to help her finish her morning-glories quilt as their farewell gift to her. While they sewed on the quilt Lizzie told them of the astonishing things she had seen while waiting for the Race to begin.

Lizzie spent the rest of the day going over her assembled goods and chattels with lists in mind and knowing everything must be prepared for Jim. The bedrolls and the box of cooking and eating utensils would be put in last. They would need at least two barrels of water. Jim would take care of the feed for the horses. She packed up her sewing kit and her almost finished quilt and lay down for a quiet rest.

"It's Papa. Come, Mama." Robbie came in yelling, Sure enough, she was just in time to see Jim trot up to the hitching rail as she opened the front door. Barney whinnied as Lizzie ran down the steps. Jim picked her up, swept her off the ground, and danced her in a little circle.

"We did it, Lizzie," he said. "We're the proud owners of a claim on the spot I remembered, one hundred and sixty acres about seven miles southwest of Alva. I found it right where I said it would be. Ott, take Barney please, and take care of him. Boy, you don't know how grateful to you I am. Wait 'til I tell you how your corn and tobacco saved our claim! What you got t'eat, Ma?"

CHAPTER 7

STARTING UP

The final touches on preparations for the trip back to Alva and the claim had taken three days. The rest had been good for Barney who was back to his usual frisky self, prancing to show off a new set of shoes. Jim and Lizzie were busy packing and loading up their big wagon so they could move as soon as possible. They knew they'd be living out of the wagon for a while so they needed to take as much as they could. After the straw mattress was placed on the bottom, Lizzie packed tin boxes of flour, sugar, coffee, corn, beans and dried meat, along with some canned goods. She loaded in the blankets, clothing and her sewing and knitting work-basket, along with cooking and eating utensils and her carefully wrapped dishes. Jim and Pa Bevis had measured and cut lumber for a table and benches, which Jim would assemble when they reached the claim. Jim packed his tools, tack and fodder for the team and Barney, and strapped a couple of extra barrels of water to the back of the wagon and they were ready to leave.

The return trip with an overnight stay at Medicine Lodge was slow. They had been on the road for several days and by the time they arrived in Alva the mud had dried into deep ruts. Ott rode on Barney, while Lizzie and little Robbie were with Jim under the new canvas cover he had bought in Pratt.

The landscape and town had changed since Jim had left over a week previously. Green grass was cropping up where only bare ground had showed before the torrential rain. Freight cars full of lumber and building materials were unloaded at the depot at Alva and the sound of sawing and hammering could be heard for quite a distance. Saloons were doing a brisk business and fisticuff fights among the patrons were commonplace. Jim looked around in amazement at the growth in population and traffic since he had left. Lizzie and Robbie too looked around them with interest as they drove through town on their way to Josh's claim to pick up Hank.

"Meet the missus," Jim nodded to Hank and Josh after he pulled up to Josh's cabin two miles east of town. "Lizzie, these are the fellers that were up at the starting line with me before the Race. Hank here is our closest neighbor and Josh over there is going to be a city dude living so close to town," Jim said, pointing his head toward Alva. Lizzie moved over to the middle of the seat while Hank climbed up into the wagon.

"I'll hold the little feller on my lap ma'am, if he don't mind," Hank smiled. "I can see he's a fine young gentleman." Robbie had no objections to climbing up on Hank's lap because he could see better when Hank pulled back the canvas on the side. Robbie pointed to the meadowlarks, prairie dogs and rabbits as they rode along. He was interested in anything that moved. Ott, who had been watering the roan at the water trough, rode up beside the wagon, waving goodbye to Josh as they started to leave.

"Josh, come see us if you can get time off from your own pioneering, y'hear," Jim said, as he raised the reins in both hands.

"You folks come by and see me on your way to town. I'll be right glad to see company unless I'm in the field a-plowin'," Josh replied.

"Giddyup," Jim commanded as he snapped the dark leather reins. "Gee, Charley" he said, trying to work the wagon out of a deep rut to the right, then pulling back on the straps to back up before turning south in the direction of his claim. It irked Jim to ride high in a wagon drawn by an unmatched team, but black Joe and gray Charley were the soundest team he could trade for his other saddle horse. They were still young enough to do the kind of plowing he wanted done, and he could maybe learn more about the art of plowing from them. Besides, they were gentle enough for Lizzie to handle if need be.

"These horses know a heap more'n I do about plowing if those strap-worn sides come about from plowing friction," Jim said to Hank.

"You're sure right about that," Hank agreed. "Nothin' else will rub the hair off'n a work horse's hide like the strainin' of plowin'."

"Milkweed will crowd out some of the grazing around here if I know the signs," Jim said. "At least they're not poison like the nightshades, and won't make the stock loco like Jimson weed," He thought of how busy he had been stocking up with supplies and gathering his family together and wondered if he forgot something.

Pa Bevis, his father-in-law, would have to go to the government land office at Alva as soon as possible if he expected to get a claim. He was grateful to Lizzie for her careful preparations. If anything had been overlooked, it would be a simple matter to get supplies at Alva since the Santa Fe train unloaded there.

As the new homesteaders drew near the claim, Ott saw Jim's banner on the white stake waving in the distance and he spurred Barney and raced ahead of the wagon so he would be the first to put foot on the claim, ahead of his sister, Lizzie.

"It sure is nice to be here, Liz," Jim exclaimed happily. "Bet you're going to like it." He smiled up at her as he reached for Robbie when the wagon stopped.

Lizzie, always the stoic, said, "Oh, it won't be too bad once we get the dugout dug and the steps laid so we can come and go in it."

"Is that all you got to say, Liz?" Jim asked, his voice revealing deep pride in his selection of a claim. "Don't you think the whole lay of the land is a cowpoke's dream come true?" He finished by adding, "I darn sure feel powerful about this quarter section, don't you Lizzie?"

Lizzie, using her affectionate pet name for him said, "Yes Jamie, I sure do." Then she added thoughtfully, "I can't put it in the proper words, but it ought to be a right fine place to raise up the children." Jim unloaded the plowshares, the churn, and the three-legged milking stool, handing them down to Hank, who made himself useful despite his bad foot.

"Pa ought to be bringing the cow in a few days," Lizzie commented. "And then we can have nice fresh milk again."

Jim and Ott unloaded the lumber already cut for the table and benches. The carpentry tools and a keg of nails and dozens of other small items that would be needed for pioneering a homestead were carefully laid aside for future use. Jim had placed sturdy garb of canvas duck fit for loggers with other heavy items. Jim knew he had to ride many miles to cut cedar posts for fencing. When everything else was unloaded, the straw tick mattress was left at the bottom of the wagon for comfort in sleeping. Lizzie had not brought the feather bed. That would come later.

"Well, Hank," Jim said when they finished unloading the wagon. "You've sure come in handy in the unloading. Take one of the buffalo hides over there to your claim. It will be a real comfort to you," Jim suggested.

Hank limped over to the small pile of hides and picked one out.

"You sure know how to pick' em, Hank," Jim said. "That's the one that gave me the most trouble and was the biggest buffalo I ever killed. Nine or ten years ago I shot him down in the Chickasaw Nation and tanned the hide myself."

Ott saddled Barney again, and went out on an inspection tour of the property. An hour later he returned from exploring the creek and looking for game.

Jim walked over to Ott, rubbed Barney's nose and said, "Ott, get off and hand the reins over to Hank. He'll ride Barney over to his claim tonight, but he'll be back for breakfast. It's too soon for him to be walking much on that foot yet.

He turned to Hank. "How's your grub holding out, Hank? Take a little hunk of this venison jerky and some of this cracking corn to keep your ribs from poking through," Jim commanded as he put the food in Hank's side pocket.

"Jim," Ott asked, "can I take the Winchester? I think I know where I can get something for dinner, a cottontail or some quail."

"Sure," Jim nodded. "Some fresh meat would be just the caper. Say, take a pail with you too, and bring back some water when you come."

Lizzie started setting up for dinner by unpacking a basket of dishes and pots and pans. Later, as they were having their dinner she said to Jim and Ott, "Just think, this is sorta a special meal. The first we're having on our new homestead. "She smiled as she held a fried saddle of rabbit in her hand. "Maybe the time will come when we'll be calling it the old homestead."

That night Ott bedded down on the other two buffalo robes underneath the wagon and tucked Robbie in beside him. Robbie had never seen a buffalo, but he had heard his father tell about them.

Lizzie and Jim lay in the wagon and talked quietly. The evening was warm and they could see the stars through the front of the wagon between the rolled back canvas flaps. Propped up, Jim smoked his pipe and looked down at her with affection as she lay beside him, arms behind her head on the pillow. He thought she never looked so lovely. Her eyes were bright with happiness. Suddenly she brought her arm down, passed her hand over her swelling stomach and knitted her eyebrows thoughtfully.

"Give me your hand, Jamie," and she placed it on her abdomen. He felt a flutter, and they both broke into an excited laugh.

"Sure feels as if he's alive and kicking," Jim whispered.

"I didn't know I was that far along. Guess it may be the end of February, instead of March. But Jim, isn't it something on our first night on our claim? Think of it, Jamie, our own home at last. Pray God we can stay here and live and grow and watch our children come up here. I don't know how you did it all."

"I couldn't have managed it without your help, honey," Jim answered. He put out his pipe, then the lantern, and they lay quietly in each other's arms, thinking and dreaming as they fell asleep looking at the stars in a land that stretched silent about them.

Morning comes early on the prairie and Lizzie stepped out of the wagon to smell the morning freshness and watch the sun come up. She was fixing a breakfast of cornmeal mush and apple butter when Hank rode up on Barney.

As they ate Jim said, "Hank, here's where you come in right handy. Let's put these shares on the plow so Ott can start tearing up the turf. I brought a tape line, and we can measure out the size of the dug-out."

He looked at Lizzie and asked her, "Have you got any mind to where you'd like your mansion in the ground?"

"Of course I have," she answered, and stepped off about thirty feet from the creek and the cottonwoods.

"It's level here," she said with satisfaction, "and will save a good many steps to water 'til we sink our well."

Lizzie was an ample woman glowing with health and vitality. Jim thought she made a pretty picture trudging over the place. She had not yet lost her shape. She stood against the cottonwoods with her shining brown hair in a soft knot, the breeze blowing little tendrils about her face. The flowered dress and the white apron above the little flat slippers were becoming to her. Jim spied Hank gazing at her with a soft look in his eyes. He grasped Hank's arm and firmly turned him away muttering about a tape line.

CHAPTER 8

THE BEVIS BUNCH

Pa Bevis had not been idle on his way from Pratt, Kansas, to the Crouch claim in Oklahoma. He had stopped in Alva in order to visit the Land Office, hoping to find some still unclaimed land. Jim's advice had impressed him with the possibilities and opportunities offered by the newly opened Territory. Nearly a week after Jim and Lizzie arrived at the claim, Pa and Levi Bevis, Jr. joined them, Pa Bevis keeping as a surprise his luck in purchasing 80 acres next to them.

Levi William Bevis was a tall man of five feet eleven inches. He had black beady eyes reminding one of glistening olives. His hair was dark brown and straight, as was his prominent long nose, which curved down at the tip. His presence was commanding. Having once met him, everyone remembered him not only for what he said, but also for what he was, a Union soldier.

As Pa Bevis drove the spring wagon up to the claim, 12-year-old Levi, Jr. held tight to the rope leading Nellie the black cow, as he had done all the way from Pratt. Nellie, tired and cross from the long trip, gave an experimental moo. When she received no answering bovine greeting, she began munching on some grass when Levi slackened the rope.

"H'lo folks, come and look at your new neighbors, the Bevis bunch!" Pa Bevis could hardly contain his excitement when Lizzie, Jim and Ott came running to greet him. "'Course, there's only two of us now, three counting Ott, but Charley and Alvin will come on the next trip to help me get started. Their Ma and Opal will stay in Kansas 'til spring."

"It's good to see that you got here all whole, Pa. The cow sure looks the worse for wear though," Lizzie said.

Pa looked at the cow. "Levi, your job ain't done 'til you take that cow down to the creek an' let her drink. Wash her off too if there's enough water in it. Calm her down before you milk her, if her udder don't bust first. Where's Ott?" Pa answered his own question, "Bet he's out hunting game. Well, hope he gets real lucky. I'm just as hungry as a bear out of hibernation."

While the supper was cooking, Pa Bevis told them about the eighty acres he had acquired kitty-cornered from them. He explained his plans for a sod house. He said that he would prefer that instead of a dugout, if they could use Jim's cellar when they saw a cyclone[1] brewing. He pointed out the advantages of the sod house, which would provide light and air, and it would form the center for many daylight activities.

"Sure, Pa," Lizzie and Jim answered in unison. "Then we'll all lend a hand to each other when it's needed," Lizzie added.

"Maybe one of the boys would like to go with me after some fence posts," Jim said, soliciting volunteers for some future time. "If I remember rightly there's a cedar grove off to the west about twenty miles. We should get there before some one else does."

That evening little Robbie had warm frothy milk, squirted directly from the cow into his little mug. Lizzie's crate of two roosters and newly laying Plymouth Rock pullets and the wire to fence them, had not been unloaded because the birds had already gone to roost. Lizzie had fed them water and dry meal when they first arrived.

"No use havin' chickens if ya can't keep 'em safe from the skunks and other varmints, like those dad-ratted coyotes," Pa said. "Guess it's too late to go inspectin' my claim tonight, but I sure want to start about dawn tomorrow."

"Take Barney, Pa," Jim urged. "It'll take forever riding those work horses if you're aiming to see all four corners. The map showed the creek running along the west, near the part closest to your line," Jim said to his father-in-law.

On that first evening on the Crouch claim, the men sat smoking and talking quietly, catching up on the news since their last meeting in Kansas. Pa Bevis looked around him, enjoying the mellow family scene with his sons Levi, Jr. and Ott, and his daughter Lizzie's family. He thought of his two sons, Charley and Alvin, still home in Pratt and how he missed them.

Eighteen-year old Charley Bevis, the eldest son, was the least serious and had the mildest temperament of all the Bevis sons. His

---

1 Cyclone, twister, tornado are used interchangeably in Oklahoma.

sense of humor made him popular at home and well liked by his friends. He was Lizzie's favorite brother. She could coax him to do things for her that Jim had neither patience nor time to do.

James Ott Bevis, always called Ott, at fourteen older than Levi Junior, was the tallest son. He was over six feet. His dark brown eyes, larger and softer than those of his father, could be equally stern on adverse occasions. Ott showed his Indian ancestry more than the other boys. His facial features were strong and open.

Levi Junior, more serious than his brother, was as forceful with matched words as his thrusting, square-cut jaw testified when anyone tried to take advantage of him.

The youngest Bevis boy, ten year old Alvin, was learning all the skills of his father and brothers

Pa Bevis was a resourceful man. He had become one of the most active horse traders in western Kansas. What he knew about horse flaws when he was the buyer was too vast for books. On the other hand, when he was the seller, he extolled their good points in flowing high praise. He was canny, sharp, and totally intent on whatever task he undertook, taking pride in coming out with the best bargain in every deal, but he also had the reputation of being a fair and honest man along with his superior knowledge of horses, learned from shoeing Army horses and from his many Civil War campaigns. His strength of character easily persuaded others to accept his offers.

At sixteen, already as mature as a man, Levi Bevis had enlisted in the Union Army in Ohio, where his family lived at the time, though they originally hailed from Kentucky. He served two enlistment terms. After being wounded in the leg, he was captured and spent the last seven months of the war in Libby Prison at Richmond. He received an honorable discharge, and came out with twelve dollars a month disability pension. His Civil War experiences had put an indelible stamp on him. He told tales of fighting every major battle from Pea Ridge, Arkansas to Vicksburg, Chickamauga, and Petersburg. Whenever he met an old war crony, he relived every battle encounter. Bevis could cuss louder and longer, and spit a cud of tobacco farther than any of his comrades. He was now one of thousands of sod busters, ready to prove up a claim in Oklahoma Territory.

Soon after his discharge from the Union Army, Levi met and wooed the lovely Alma Tower, who was of English descent. Her first American ancestor, Puritan John Tower, came from England in 1633. In 1637 he helped found Hingham, Massachusetts. A later Tower ancestor fought in the French and Indian wars. A Gideon Tower fought in both the Revolution and in the War of 1812. Alma was a true Daughter of the Revolution. Her daughter Lizzie inherited her usually forebearing character. Her second daughter, Vena, called Veny, took more after her father in appearance and disposition. Veny had left home early determined to seek her own future and fortune independently. Bright, pretty, nine-year old Opal was the baby of the family.

The life of a horse trader required many changes. It was a chore for Alma each time the Bevis family moved. In addition to organizing the complexity of the actual move, she had to find shelter for her brood of seven living children. Three of her children had died; her eldest son William, her daughter Rosalind, and a newborn baby. Will, her first-born, the idol of the whole family, died of typhoid at the age of nineteen, a sorrow that remained with the whole family.

More than anything on earth, having a place of her own on which to settle down without further thought of moving would suit Alma. During the twenty-four years of waiting, bearing and rearing children had been her chief interest. Until the Run for land in 1893 she had carried a feeling that a home of her own was all but impossible. "If somehow we could acquire a piece of that free land, then this eternal roaming would cease." She had urged her husband to get a homestead.

Many years before, the family had started in Indiana, crossed Illinois and Missouri, and in 1893 were living in Kansas. They were a family of traders, living off their wits, asking no favors and giving no quarter. Now, at last, Pa Bevis had staked their claim, and God willing, Ma Bevis would join them once Opal's and Alvin's school year ended in April of 1894.

Alma grieved over Veny's quarrel with her father. No child of his had ever defied him without getting horsewhipped. When Veny had been hired out to a well-to-do family in Pratt, Pa said she took on fancy notions.

When she came home to get her clothes she said to her father, "I aim to leave permanently. There's free land down near Guthrie in the Oklahoma Territory. I intend to get a piece of it and I know some folks who are ridin' in on the train, so I'll go with them."

Her father was sorely displeased. Veny was emphatic and stamped her foot in response to his protests.

"If you go, Veny, you're no longer a daughter of mine!" he thundered at her. "Furthermore, don't come back here asking for your room and board."

Then he added with fatherly concern, "Look out for them slick talkin' fellers. They delight in encitin' young women away from home, then desert 'em when they're through with 'em."

"Why Pa," she replied, "you got it all wrong. I'm goin' with the Gobels. Ben and Jenny are friends of the Schaffers, all nice folks. Besides, I'm twenty-one now and I'm my own boss."

***

So far the Indian summer had persisted late into October. The days raced by and the men discussed the farming, the planting and the crops. Thanksgiving came and went with less than the usual amount of attention from the busy group, and the families enjoyed a hearty meal together. The day provided a time to rest and a pause for breath in the business of getting things done before the winter really hit the prairie. Only since the middle of November had the cold become uncomfortable in the early mornings.

The dugout, started at the beginning of October was completed in the first couple of weeks. Lizzie hung crochet curtains so she felt a degree of comfort in the otherwise bare surroundings. It felt good to come up from the dugout during the day, and equally good to sit around the fire in the evenings. Life was taking on an aspect of order. Lizzie felt a peace and contentment that she always dreamed of, but never had before. She was unhampered by her pregnancy and at times delighted in working the team to clear the ground in preparation for the tillage of the soil.

The sod house was finished by the beginning of November. Pa Bevis was pleased to find some glass for the windows at the railhead in Alva from a neighbor who had received a little more than he had needed. The price had been reasonable and Pa Bevis was delighted to have a bargain.

Another joy had entered Lizzie's life in the coming of Ellie Hartner. The two became friends almost at once and shared many tasks, as did their men. Ellie was bright and cheerful and her sense of fun did much to lighten the hard work. She told Lizzie she would never forget the welcome the Crouches afforded her upon her arrival, in addition to Jim's kindness to Hank at the time of the Race. Ellie looked forward to the birth of her first child, knowing that Lizzie, her new friend and neighbor lived close by.

CHAPTER 9

THE LOAN

Early in December of 1893, on one of his rare visits into town, Jim stopped by Josh Montgomery's claim. As he drove in, he was looking at Josh's matched work team tied up in front of his newly completed frame house.

Jim got down from the wagon and hitched his unmatched team next to Josh's handsome pair. Josh stepped out the front door to greet him and Jim looked around him in amazement.

"Say Josh," Jim jokingly asked him, "did you find a gold mine in your back yard or something? I see as how you're copying those city dudes and even starting a new barn. You've been here just a bit over two months and look at you! Bet you got aholt of one of them town carpenters to help you."

Josh ignored Jim's teasing and instead questioned him, "How's yer place comin'? Have ya got yer winter wheat planted yet?"

"Yep, we're planting it now and I had to come to town to get some more seed," Jim answered. "I'm afraid I'm a reckless speculator. You see, I'm getting strapped for cash. Figure if I can get a loan I can pay it off and have some money left for more improving after selling the first crop. They say there's a new bank in Alva now. The weather has been awful nice and if it keeps favorable, we can make it all right."

"Well, Jim, did ya get your dugout digged? And how's Hank a-comin'?" Josh asked in the same breath.

"To answer your first question, my wife's ole man, Pa Bevis, and three of his four sons came and he put them all to work. We got ours dug and then they built a mighty fine big sod house on their eighty acre claim next to me and Hartner. Hank's wife, Ellie and younger brother Howie, drove in, loaded down so heavy with supplies that the horses could hardly pull the wagon. Took 'em about ten days to get here from Iowa. And that was going some."

Jim tipped his hat back on his head and grinned at Josh.

"Ellie is expecting same time as Lizzie," Jim continued, "and they'll be acting as midwife for each other. Hank sure wants a son.

If it weren't for Hank, Liz's Pa and me wouldn't know exactly how to put in our wheat crops. He sure is a mighty fine neighbor."

Josh nodded in agreement. Then, looking seriously at Jim, he changed the subject.

"Jim, don't you try goin' to those banks or loan outfits for money when you got a friend like me."

"Josh," Jim said keeping his voice light, "I didn't come here for cripes sake, looking for any loan from you. Didn't know you had any rum profits left after this long. But looking at the lay of your land now I can see I overlooked your talents! Bet it was all planned that you would become a loan shark yourself."

"Jim, you old buzzard," Josh answered, ignoring Jim's sarcasm. "Can't ya get it through your fool head that I want to do ya a favor? Hell, you won't have to draw up no fancy papers! I'll only charge ya four percent a year interest. Your word is the only bond I need. I trust ya Jim, mor'n anyone I can remember. How much will you be needin'?"

Jim looked at Josh long enough to see Josh meant what he said.

"I'll take you up on that," Jim replied. "Could you make it an even two hundred? But if that would cramp you, I could do with a hundred and fifty. Thanks, Josh, I didn't know what a good friend you really was."

When Jim pulled his team out of Montgomery's yard into the clod-strewn road, he had two hundred in ten double eagles in his pocket. His mind harkened back to Josh's last words. "Let's keep this transaction quiet. Don't want more loanin' business than I can handle." Then suddenly, a terrible thought struck Jim, and he said aloud, "No, no, Josh wouldn't hurt anyone." Jim's habit of talking to himself returned, as it always did when he was troubled. "Before I get out my detective spy-glass, I mustn't jump to conclusions. I must be real careful in asking Hank, casual like, just how the stabbing outside the saloon tent came about that day."

Darkness had settled before Jim drove up to the side of the dugout and halted the team where he could unload handily. Everyone was out to greet him, all talking at once. Lizzie could tell that he was successful in his endeavors, so she said nothing, knowing he would share his venture with her when the appropriate time arrived. Jim handed a stick of lemon candy to Robbie, and gave a stick of peppermint to Ott, who had hung around after the unloading knowing he would receive some treat. Lizzie was given the pink striped paper bag containing the rest of the ten cents worth of rock candy that she preferred.

***

Everybody was busy with chores. Ellie and Lizzie spent a great deal of time sewing these days. Ellie had brought an old pedal Wilcox-Wheeler chain-stitching sewing machine along with her. It was indeed a prize gift from her mother. It enabled the two ladies-in-waiting to accomplish the many tasks to prepare for the eagerly anticipated babies, as well as to make their homes more comfortable. Jim reflected back to his youth on the old plantation in Kentucky. The women and slaves had sewn only by hand and most of the yardage was either woven on the place, or came from eastern ports. The availability of technology and transportation had leaped forward in this newly settled country. One could see it everywhere: the railroad, the farm implements, and the mail-order catalog that could supply any reasonable order in house wares and fabrics and notions. Life was moving fast.

Jim and Hank planted the winter wheat when the days were short, with the weather blustery on occasion. They consulted the Farmer's Almanac almost daily for information, and had planted seed potatoes in the dark of the moon according to the instructions. What a source of security that publication was to the new homesteaders in the Cherokee Strip that winter.

On a fine crisp winter day near the end of 1893, Jim and Hank walked towards the creek to locate a site to witch water[1] for a well. The light wind turned the last of the leaves from the cottonwoods lining the creek.

"Hank," Jim asked as they walked, "remember when you were relating about that stabbing outside the saloon tent in Alva, when I was racing back to Kansas the day we registered our claims? I'd like to hear more about it again. At the time when you were first telling it to me, Ott was listening with all ears and I didn't want

---

1 Water witching or dowsing is the art of finding water underground using a forked stick, preferably

taken from a willow tree. A rod or pendulum can also be used.

him to get all soaked up in crime. You know how boys can get the wrong ideas!"

Jim slowed his pace and turned sideways to look at Hank. "Did I understand you right, that Josh left you in the saloon to rest your leg while he went to buy something?"

"Well, I didn't exactly say he did," Hank answered slowly, trying to remember, "but I guess that's about the way it was."

"Then Josh returned in about twenty minutes to half an hour and hollered to you to come, that he found a man outside moaning?" Jim asked. "Isn't that so Hank? Do you recall about what time it was when the braggart left the saloon?"

"Well," Hank answered, scratching his head, "think it was soon after Josh left. We all heard the thunder 'n lightnin' and I suppose he just wanted to get goin' like we all did."

Jim stopped walking altogether and faced Hank.

"Hank, I guess I ought to explain that I thought of becoming a lawman myself. Read some books on how detectives solve crimes but concluded that I wasn't tough enough. 'Fraid I'm too softhearted and might get my sympathy worked-up in favor of the criminal, and you know a good lawman can't do that! Besides, I'm a very poor shot and don't believe in wearing a gun. And then, it's a dangerous game. Very few lawmen live much beyond forty, outlaws either. Luck has to be with them, on either side of the law. Afraid my luck would of run out if I switched to anything but riding and homesteading. No cowpuncher wants to die in bed, it's a reckless life too. But I just don't hanker to die with my boots on so soon, so I gave up the notion to be a lawman."

Hank nodded his understanding. They started walking again, but Jim was so busy thinking about the stabbing he forgot about the willow twig sticking out of his hip pocket to witch for water.

"Tell me, Hank," Jim continued, "do you think the victim was dead when you helped to hoist him up over the rump of the stranger's mount? 'Course I'm getting the cart before the horse. Do you think he had any right to take a wounded man away without first reporting it to the federal marshal? Did you ever stop to think, Hank, that the dark stranger who appeared out of the storm so suddenly might-a bin the intended victim, or even the murderer himself? And he just come back to remove the evidence, the corpus delictus?"

"Jim, slow down." Hank said peevishly. "You don't give me time to answer a one of yer questions. Yes, the victim was alive, but barely breathin'. His chest was bleedin' somethin' terrible 'til his so-called pal stuck a fancy bandanna in the wound. The storm made the sky black with clouds and it weren't easy to see, 'cept with the lightnin' flashes. When he was alayin' on the ground, I seen a deep slash right between the front ribs like it could-a bin done by a switch blade or a huntin' knife. I recognized him at once as the braggart from the saloon. I'm sure I never seen the dark stranger afore. He looked at me and said, "Make way, boy, this fella is a pal o' mine. I'll take over if you'll lend me a hand to get him to a doctor."

"So I helped him," Hank continued. "The first thing he did though, was to ransack the man's pockets and bemoan that a cussed renegade must-a got off with his gold swag. That's why I didn't think it was him that done it."

"Could of been play-acting, criminals can be razor-sharp," Jim said as he stared at the sky while the sun lowered itself to the horizon. "Supposing he was a criminal? Maybe he wasn't. We can only speculate. I don't want to be accusing an innocent man. Maybe the braggart wasn't a villain either. In any case he ought not to get a mortal wound for showing a gold double eagle. Honest men have that kind of money too. I had a few myself before I made the Race and had to use some to buy two-by-four timber for bracing the dugout, and other things that we couldn't do without."

Jim turned to Hank and asked, "Wasn't Josh about to send you to the marshal's office before the stranger rode up?"

"I couldn't go no place with my foot," Hank replied. "Josh said he was 'bout to report it. The unlucky victim looked like he was done in fer good. In time I suppose I'd-a thought of goin' myself. 'Course I wasn't expectin' a thing like any stabbin' that first day in town."

"One thing's for sure," opined Jim. "What chance he had of surviving in the position he was riding in was slim."

Jim and Hank noticed suddenly how late it was getting and headed back towards the soddy.

"How could a feller find out if anyone was missin', Jim? Why, we don't know the scalawag's name, or where he hails from."

Jim spoke up, "It sure seems to be a puzzle. Fact of the matter is, we couldn't even prove there was a stabbing as far as evidence goes. The corpus delictus is missing, that's what the courts of law call the body. We don't rightly know but what the unlucky bounder might of recovered. Hope to God he did! I didn't see no buzzards circling around on the trail to the Kansas border on the return trip down here."

He clapped his hand on Hank's shoulder. "Guess we better keep this whole mystery to ourselves. We ain't got time to be questioned by the law. I know, Hank, you done your duty so far as you knew it, that's for sure."

That night, troubled in his mind, Jim lay awake a long time. He had taken a two-hundred dollar loan from Josh Montgomery, and had spent half of it already. It was true that he had borrowed the money in good faith. His suspicions that the money might be tainted were not aroused until later. In questioning Hank he had not discovered anything to relieve his mind that Josh was not physically involved in the stabbing. Contrariwise, he became more suspicious than ever.

Each cowboy was stamped with a moral code of his own and he adhered to his unique set of ethics. Call it pride or superstitious fancy, some cowboys would prefer to starve rather than ride with an outfit that preyed on the weakness of others. Jim Crouch firmly believed that ill-gotten gains brought nothing but disaster or ruin to those who engaged in robbery, bribery, and worst of all, violence and murder. He decided to arrange for a loan from the bank so he could return the entire amount to Josh. He strongly suspected that Josh had either murdered or attempted to murder the braggart after he left the bar.

Jim did not have an opportunity to go into town to the bank. The winter was about them and the snows came to draw a mantle of white on the prairie. The year drew to a close and the plains slept to prepare for the reawakening of the blessed spring.

CHAPTER 10

THE ACCIDENT

One morning just before dawn, the noisy arrival of Levi, Jr. with his wagon woke the still sleeping Jim, who hurriedly dressed and went out to hitch up his own wagon and team. He had forgotten he had arranged with young Levi for them to drive twenty miles west to the cedar breaks to cut down trees for fenceposts. Thus began the day that eventually changed the course of his life, that of his family, and the future of the claim itself.

They arrived at the grove of widely scattered cedars, most of them not over twelve to fourteen feet high. They set to work felling several of the largest ones and by the time they stopped for their noon meal the second buckboard was almost half full.

After eating and resting a bit they went back to work. Jim had almost finished cutting one of the larger trees when it suddenly snapped and fell the wrong way catching his right hand, throwing him off-balance to the ground, and twisting his right leg. The tree smashed down on his right hand, crushing the index finger flat from the knuckle to the tip.

Levi, Jr. ran over to him, moving the tree with new-found strength and helped Jim struggle to his feet. Jim quickly wrapped his neckerchief around his hand and limped to his buckboard, climbing awkwardly to the seat. Despite the excruciating pain he hurried his team towards home, gripping the reins tightly in his left hand with Levi, Jr. following close behind with the other team.

Arriving at Jim's home, Levi, Jr. leapt from his wagon and ran to help Jim into the dugout, then ran to his own home to tell his father about the accident. Pa Bevis came over with a draft of home-distilled brandy and pressed his son-in-law to drink it down. A few teaspoons were left to cauterize the wound after the liquor took effect on Jim. Lizzie's face showed her concern and sympathy as she prepared a lean meat poultice, placed it around the badly injured finger, then wrapped it with a clean cloth. If a doctor had been available he probably would have amputated it as the knuckle was crushed flat.

For several days and nights Jim had little or no sleep. He had never known such torment. For a while they worried about blood poisoning setting in, but he was spared that problem. Every day one of the boys killed a rabbit and Lizzie repeated her fresh meat poultices. Slowly his hand began to heal, but as time passed the finger began to stiffen and the use of his hand was greatly impaired.

To him the accident confirmed his own superstition that the borrowed money was tainted. The notion that the money had brought him ill luck persisted, but he dared not voice his suspicions, even to Lizzie, so he suffered both in body and in mind.

One big relief to Jim was the devotion shown to him by his brothers-in-law and Hank in taking care of the farm work while he was recuperating. Ott and Levi, Jr. kept up with all the chores, even milking the cow for Lizzie as her movements became more awkward.

Hank came over and watched for signs of sprouts in the winter wheat crop. The boys took direction and did men's work, learning as they worked. The workhorses had to be shod, a chore at which Pa Bevis excelled. Ott declared he would become a blacksmith himself. The anvil, the red hot irons, the working of the bellows, together with handling a horse convinced him that only a superior man could do that kind of work. Ott knew that in a year or two he would be strong enough to work as a blacksmith. In the meantime he would go on learning the skills of the trade.

Jim continued to mend in mind, body and spirit, a quiet time during which the only benchmark was the birth of their second son. Freddy arrived in February, 1894.

Ten days later Hank got the son he wanted, Henry, Jr. and declared, "an' nobody's goin' to call him anything but Henry." Life was changing around the Crouch menage. The dugout was getting too crowded but would have to make do for at least another two years. Jim did not want to spend the remaining hundred dollars, yet had not felt equal to a showdown with Josh. He was waiting until he got paid for the harvested wheat. He reckoned he would take the whole two hundred dollars over and pay Josh the entire four percent interest for the year, even if the loan had six months to go. That would ease his conscience some.

The Come-See Child

It was not the winter blizzard that
blighted my debut, roaring;
Nor was it the old crone who cut
my umbilical cord.
It was not the starry heaven o'er me that
Shone of its own accord,
But it was my spirit soaring,
Leaving ivory palaces for earthly limits
In the shape of flesh and blood.

***

Gladys Iris Crouch Clark

CHAPTER 11

THE COME-SEE CHILD

When the spring rains of 1895 came the roof leaked and the dugout was frightfully damp and most uncomfortable. Baby Freddy, a year old now, got rain-splashed just like all of the others. He cried and sneezed, then developed a cold and fever. When his symptoms persisted and his hacking cough became worse, Lizzie bundled him up and had Jim drive them the seven miles to see the doctor in Alva. The physician prescribed a mixture of paregoric, tar and horehound. When it was filled Lizzie gave some to the fretting child.

While making a few purchases, Jim and Lizzie chatted with the owner of the newly framed store. An old crone came hobbling over on a crooked cane. She wanted to see the 'wee bairn.' When Lizzie later related the unnerving experience to Ellie, she described the woman as near ninety, with skimpy long white hair, her face a map of wrinkles, and smelling of the old cob pipe she was smoking.

"I'm Granny Sullivan, and I've second sight. Some say I'm a witch, but don't ya believe it! Your laddie is a little angel too good for this silly world. He's a 'come-see child.' I only tell what I see, or what the good Lord puts in my mind to say. Sure an' since I were a wee lass back in auld Erin, I could see the Little People, but I don't have no truck with sorcery. Come an' see me sometime. I'm livin' wid me youngest daughter, Maureen. Her man is Mike Mulcahy, in Liberty Township, due south o' here."

Lizzie asked, "What do you mean, a come-see child? Never heard no expression like that before!"

"An angel babe with a guardian angel standin' in the back, waitin' to take him back when he's seen enuf," Granny Sullivan answered with a far away look in her eyes.

Lizzie felt a cold chill run up and down the length of her entire body. She had her own fleeting superstitions. She had voiced them to nobody, keeping her own counsel, and since Jim's accident, especially not to him. She knew something was aggravating her husband and from experience she knew she would have to bide her time until he was ready to share with her what he had on his mind. She was reluctant to add to his burden her fears about Freddy.

The prescription helped Freddy, who recovered after three days to again go trailing after Robbie. Her routine of spring cleaning, farm chores, cooking and hoeing took Lizzie's mind off the dire prophecy. She would not have dwelled on the incident even if she had recalled it. Lizzie placed her faith in doctors and medicine, rather than in second sight.

When the abundant spring showers ceased, the cacti and flowers on the sod house roof, which had taken root and filled in the cracks and crannies, suddenly burst forth in a profusion of bright colors. Red, yellow and orange cactus blossoms, and blue and purple wild flowers covered the roof.

Opal Bevis clapped her hands gleefully and said to her mother, "Look Ma! The prettiest house on the prairie. It's grand, with flowers on the roof like quality folks get, only they have to hang them in those little baskets. Ours just grow!"

Opal had her rag doll to play with, but now she was able to play dolls with real live babies. Although just four years older than Robbie, she assumed a protective attitude towards her big sister's children and she was left alone with them when it was necessary.

Once when she and Robbie were playing outside, Opal went to the dugout to check on Freddy in his cradle. She found a coiled rattlesnake on the top landing. She ran directly to the garden where Lizzie was hoeing and hollered "Bring your hoe! There's a rattler on the steps!"

Lizzie sprinted to the dugout and swung her hoe down hard hitting the snake right behind the head and decapitating it in two blows. She picked up the severed head with a pitchfork and burned it in the kitchen fire. She told the children it was always necessary to do this. A person could step on a rattler's tooth, and still be poisoned from the poison sac inside the severed skull. Even a buried head was unsafe. She picked up the body, twirling it by the tail, commenting that it would make good eating for the Indians. The snakeskin and rattles she would tan and cure. Lizzie liked to show off her talents to her husband and she meant to keep the hide for a hatband or a belt for him.

Opal nodded her head like a wise old owl and resumed her baby-sitting unperturbed. On Tuesdays Opal went to Ellie's soddy to take care of baby Henry while Ellie did her outside chores. The women of the frontier learned to depend upon one another at an early age.

During the winter spent in Pratt, Opal had knitted, and Ma Bevis had tatted lace, and crocheted curtains and antimacassars. Upon her arrival at the Bevis claim, Ma Bevis hung up her curtains and put the antimacassars in place on chairs. These additions did a great deal to make the sod house more homey and comfortable.

Pa Bevis bought a few pigs. As they were unloaded he proclaimed, "No coyote is goin' to tackle any of them, particularly that sow, with her squeal as loud as a dog itself!"

Just before the harvest, towards the end of May, Pa announced, "It's hog killin' time folks, we gotta have meat for the harvesters."

The threshing started on Jim's claim first, a bit earlier than he had calculated. The grain was well headed and full grained. The Red Turkey wheat crop proved ample justification of the risk Jim took in borrowing money for extra seed. Unfortunately, Jim had to wait for the completion of the granary at Alva. Meanwhile, prices dropped on the Chicago Board of Trade owing to the report of a bumper crop. The law of supply and demand operated even across great distances. Homesteading could be frustrating at times. Pa Bevis had paid seventy dollars for his good spring wagon. Jim had paid a hundred twenty-five dollars for the seed. The loan would be four percent. The harvesters would be paid between seventy-five and eighty cents a day with board and room. The way the harvest looked, Jim would do well to get eighty cents or so per bushel for his wheat. Jim shook his head and told himself to quit worrying about it. Actually he would be doing all right when his profits were figured. This was only his second year, and he would already be free and clear, so to speak.

When Jim finally deposited his crop after hauling it to the town granary, he was pleased to discover he had more profit than he had calculated. Right after purchasing supplies he drove out to Montgomery's place, intending to pay off his loan and interest to Josh. Nobody was about, and the house looked deserted. The business would have to wait until his return to town in another week. Jim had gone to the new First National Bank and made considerable transactions with the agreeable banker, Mr. Nichols. The gold pieces had been converted into two, one hundred dollar bills. These yellow notes guaranteed that they were convertible to gold. Jim felt the jinx of tainted money in his possession was broken. Now he could afford to wait.

Josh had not returned within the week when Jim drove by again. With no livestock the claim looked deserted. No one knew what had caused Josh to leave: only Jim suspected the nature of his absence. Josh had hidden out before when things got hot.

***

The winter of 1895 arrived and Jim planted the third crop of wheat. The homestead area of the claim was permanently fenced and there was a corral built next to the new barn. Occupying an unneeded space in the front yard, a buggy shed did double duty as a tack room and a dry storage place for sacks of chicken feed and the sweepings of the wheat. Wall hooks held frequently used hand tools.

The Crouches bought a few pigs. Though they added to the work and needed swill, Nellie usually had plenty of milk left over, except when she went dry in the late spring. After her twin heifer calves were born she came in fresh again. The hens roosted in the barn. Robbie and little Freddy, who was walking about, liked to gather eggs with their mother.

Lizzie learned how to cut corners from her neighbor Ellie, who had a puritanical sense of order declaring that God made the universe to run in an orderly manner. Though Lizzie learned a great deal from her association with Ellie, she was unable to organize herself to conform to the children's requirements, much less to their increasing demands on her time and efforts.

One of the ways Ellie devised to stretch her dimes was to set aside a patch of ground for a small barley crop. After Hank had plowed the field, planted the seed and harvested the barley, a part was sold and some traded to her neighbors for whatever surpluses they had, such as sorghum, duck's eggs or anything else. Ellie told Lizzie that barley was a necessary product.

Coffee was 10 cents a pound for roasted beans, but less for unroasted ones. She thought that was too great a luxury for them to drink straight. Ellie therefore placed a layer of barley on a cookie sheet and roasted it in a slow oven at the same time she roasted the coffee beans. When they reached a golden brown color she set them aside to cool before grinding them together. The brew it made was not only just as aromatic, but more mellow without a bitter aftertaste. Like other housewives in the Strip, Ellie made hard times coffee, by adding a tablespoon of powdered chickory to this concoction.

The Hartners ate barley porridge for breakfast. Made just like oatmeal, it was soaked an hour or so before boiling. The family drank barley water that had stood for three days until almost reached a fermenting stage. Ellie believed it had some medicinal value especially for curing babies' colic or when their stomachs seemed distressed.

"Barley grounds make better compost than straight coffee grounds. That's one of the things the hogs don't get," Ellie remarked.

Lizzie learned to mix the coffee and barley grounds with the chicken manure to fertilize the garden as Ellie did. After awhile the soil improved until they could grow strawberries. They also grew raspberries and currants, which they dried to take the place of raisins.

Lizzie and Ellie were catching up on their mending while talking and planning about their fast-approaching dual confinement, when Ellie put down her sewing and turned to Lizzie.

"You know Lizzie", she said with a sigh, "I do kinda hate to have another baby in the winter".

"I know what you mean, Ellie, Lizzie replied with a smile, but I know I'll get along better this time now that Ma is living close by, and she's real experienced. I just know she'll be mighty glad to do anything she can for you an' Hank and Henry when your time comes too. Hank has been so much help with our wheat crops, that it'll be a labor of love rather than a duty. You know Ellie, Jim's hand is still real troublesome to him. Guess we didn't realize all of the things he was used to doing with his right hand!"

Ellie nodded her understanding. Both sewed quietly for awhile.

"How does Hank feel about the new arrival?" Lizzie finally asked.

"Well, of course Hank wants another boy for help on the farm. They figger wives don't need girls for extra help in the kitchen and everything else we do. Guess we wimmin folks'll just have to have a flock of both kinds to get the help we need for farm work inside and outside!"

"I hear you!" Lizzie exclaimed with a smile. "but I'm so happy about this one I'm carryin' I don't care if it's a boy or a girl. Already I can tell the good Lord is sending one of his best."

CHAPTER 12

TOGETHER

The 1896 Christmas season approached and the serenity of winter had once more spread across the land. The livestock were under shelter in their stalls in the new barn. The abundant summer harvest had allowed them to add more money to their house fund, and baby Gladys, at almost a year old, was chasing after her brothers. This would be a time for celebration. Jim talked it over with Pa Bevis.

"The dugout and the covered wagon are too crowded for putting up another soul," Jim said. "My pa hasn't seen this part of the country since he moved to Kiowa on the quarter section he bought near there. I'd like him to see my new family. Do you think your boys could sleep on pallets and let Pa and Sill sleep at your place? Lizzie thinks you would."

"Why of course we would," Pa Bevis answered. "I'd be right honored to have him share our humble hearth, the whole tribe of them."

During the planning and reaching out to bring the families together for the holiday season Jim gave no thought to the opposite perceptions of the Civil War, or to the post war sentiments of the two patriarchs.

A crisp snow had fallen the night before Jim's father and step-mother arrived. The sky was overcast while the wind howled unabated. The long journey from the train station at Alva was cold and frosty. The chill reached to the very marrow of the traveler's bones. For once little Harry was glad to cuddle up to his twin brother Ray for warmth during the two hour ride to the Bevis claim. "It's a long, long way to go for Christmas when we have our own little family and things at home for comfort, without going out in the cold like this," Priscilla remarked petulantly to Charley Bevis as he drove the wagon. Sill had lost nothing of her usual self-interest.

Jim welcomed them warmly when they arrived at the Bevis soddy, "Sill, you look as young and pretty as ever," he commented graciously to his stepmother. "Your boys must not give you any worry, looking so young-like! I'm real sorry that Earl didn't come with you."

"Well," she answered rather aloofly, "they don't if Ray lets Harry have everything he wants first. Harry is very precocious," she continued. "I suppose we should not allow him to treat Ray the way he does," she concluded in a rather vague tone. "Earl is staying with my sister Ada."

Lizzie took Sill's hand when there was no move to accept a welcome hug. Sill could not forget that Lizzie had once worked for her as a hired girl. Besides, she was not sure of the blood strain. She recalled the rumor that Lizzie could have Indian blood. 'Jim sure got himself into it,' she thought to herself.

Every female in the Bevis and Crouch clans was put to work under the supervision of Ma Bevis. She was used to cooking for ten people daily, not to mention the extra mouths that would appear at harvest time, but this celebration called for the women's combined talents and ingenuity. They had made suet puddings and mince pies to put on the pie shelf Charlie had built for his mother. Fruitcake with prunes, raisins and candied peel made two weeks previously now reposed carefully wrapped on a pantry shelf. In the early summer they had made red sand plum syrup along with a dozen glasses of jelly from the tart fruit. For this occasion, they prepared a tasty punch from the syrup.

Opal ran errands back and forth from the sod house to the Crouch dugout, while she did a hundred chores for her mother and sister.

"If your sister Veny could be here with us my cup would be full." Ma Bevis sighed, then added, "Did I tell you she's engaged to be married? Some carpenter, by the name of Milt. She has such high-flyin' notions I hope he can hold her down to earth!"

"Did you bring her letter, Ma?" Lizzie asked her. "What did Pa say?"

"Oh, no, child. I didn't mention the letter to him! Charlie slipped it in to me."

Lizzie shook her head slowly, but said nothing. When the preparations were almost complete the two women sat down to rest for a few minutes while a pot of vegetables cooked. They surveyed their handiwork, and the table with the decorations which the youngsters had put out. Lizzie said, "Oh Ma, the table looks beautiful."

A short time later everyone sat down to Christmas dinner. There were extra chairs about the festive board and many improvised seats. Some of the little ones had pillows or something extra to provide a boost to reach the table. Pa Bevis said grace and pronounced blessings, offering gratitude for the horn of plenty and for peace among men. Everyone had a large portion of turkey and of the other delicious dishes. Ma Bevis smiled and looked around proudly.

"The gobbler was the homegrown variety," she said.

"The spuds are homegrown too, most everything is, including the cabbage for the coleslaw." Ott spoke with a beaming smile, which belied his recollection of the hard work in the garden in the heat.

"How's Keene, Pa?" Jim asked, then turned to his father-in-law, querying him, "You never met my brother did you?"

Pa Crouch answered, before Pa Bevis could respond.

"He's doing fine. Raising pigs and jacks[1], the finest you ever saw. His wheat yields the most of any place around Capron. He's getting rich already with no one to spend it on, and still a bachelor with no matrimonial prospects. At least there's no woman who interests him right now. The U. S. Army buys all the mules he can raise, and jacks are fetching a good price now."

Before the fruitcake with hot brandy sauce was served, Pa Bevis asked how the elder Crouch compared his Kansas farm to his Kentucky plantation.

"There's a lot of difference," Pa Crouch said. "The plantation was running good before the war. We had Negro slaves, very obedient they were, too. But many of us plantation owners wanted to avoid the war we could see coming so, like others, we voluntarily set our slaves free, any who wanted to go. They all left except for one older couple, Ossie and Martha. Kept them 'til they died. Buried them right on the old place."

---

1 Jacks are male mules.

"It sure is a dastardly shame the rest of the plantation owners in the south didn't give their slaves freedom," Pa Bevis said emphatically. "There wouldn't have been no need of that unbearable war with the cream of the country dead, or crippled, and their hate and vengeance still a-rottin' their minds."

"I'm afraid you don't know all the facts," Pa Crouch answered. "That was a political war pure and simple. You had a subsidized Congress," he continued, "too weak to see what a contentious Secretary of War Stanton was. He had Lincoln bamboozled too! Lincoln found out too late. For the last two years of the war he was willing to negotiate a settlement between the States. That canny old fox Stanton and the munitions makers had him hypnotized to their way of thinking. Everyone had his ax to grind!"

Pa Bevis interrupted indignantly, his voice rising, "Are you tellin' me that I fought all those bloody battles, Pea Ridge, Shilo, Chickamauga, and got this bullet," Bevis paused to lift his leg and pointed to the injured area before he drew breath and continued, "just because them industrialists wanted to get rich?"

"Of course there's a lot more to it than that, Bevis," Pa Crouch said, his annoyance with Pa Bevis beginning to show. "Let me ask you how old you were when you enlisted? Fifteen or sixteen weren't you? How much did you know about the situation when you enlisted? Very little, I'm sure. There were plenty of inequities on both sides, and jealousies too. You will admit that. But the worst gall for the south to take was The Emancipation Proclamation that freed the southern slaves, but did not free them for four of the northern states!"

For a few moments Pa Bevis's Union loyalties made him almost forget that he was host to the old Kentuckian. Because he didn't have a ready answer to the Southerner's difference of opinion about the North, he managed to hold his tongue.

"Bevis, you had your losses and misfortunes, but we had ours beyond description," Pa Crouch continued. "Our plantation was burned out from under us. Our land was scarred where the fighting actually took place. And you do know, don't you, that except for Gettysburg most of the major battles occurred on Southern soil. So was most of the day-to-day fighting. Our food and valuables confiscated, our sense of dignity vilified, the carpetbagger invasion later, leaving us destitute and without hope of recovery."

He took a deep breath and then said, "I'm afraid you never considered there was another side to the most horrible war of all time. You and I will never get over what it did to each of us personally. We will have to bear it. But what it did to our once glorious nation is something that is beyond repair. Our children's children will, in some way, be paying for it five hundred years from now! Well, I guess I've said enough!" And with that Pa Crouch started eating his dessert, oblivious to the sudden silence in the room.

Pa Bevis sent a glowering look Lizzie's way, saw the pleading in her big brown eyes and kept his quiet.

Lizzie gently changed the subject. "Remember when we finish at the table there are gifts for the children. The boys have been whittlin' on things that I'm sure Ray and Harry will like and there's one to take home to Earl. Of course someone had to stay home with poor Ada until she got over her pleurisy, but it must be a dull holiday for Earl."

Seizing the opportunity, Priscilla spoke up. "That's why we must get an early dawn start tomorrow to see how my sister and our first-born son are doing."

Ma Bevis drew a sigh of relief, knowing that a quick flare-up of temper on Pa's part could have had a disastrous effect on the whole Christmas spirit. As it was, from that day forward, no one ever mentioned another plan to get the Crouch and Bevis clans together again, nor did the elder Crouch ever return to visit his own son Jim's claims. Never again did those two grand old men meet, the one whose sympathies embraced the cause of the Confederate States, and the other, a Union soldier who had spilled his blood on the battlefields until finally he was taken prisoner at Petersburg, Virginia. Until the end of the war he was interned at Libby Prison, enduring indescribable hardships in a hellhole even worse than Andersonville.

The Civil War had been over for thirty years. Yet that generation did not forget its horrors for a moment, nor did they shift their loyalties and sympathies one iota. The war had ruptured the hearts and minds of the participants. Like a festering sore, it refused to heal. Perhaps the next generation might grieve less. Many Civil War veterans sincerely espoused the philosophy that the hurt would never heal.

***

One bright spring day in 1897 Hank heard the chirp of the first red-breasted robin and noticing the antics of a blue jay he was reminded that he should take a look at Jim's spring wheat field. His own was doing right well as he had planted it a week earlier than Crouch. He had never once forgotten that his little empire, as he pictured it to himself, would not have existed except for Jim's hard decision to make the claim possible. Gratitude was a quality that possessed Hank to the core of his being. He could never do enough for Jim to repay him for the use of the horse, which enabled him to find his claim on the morning following the Race. And later, for getting him to the land office in his injured state to register his claim. Likewise, he yearned to repay Josh Montgomery for having taken charge of him while his foot was still badly injured, for giving him shelter in the storm, and for feeding him while he was without funds.

"Jim, what do you suppose has happened to Josh? Don't look natural for a man to build a house and barn, plow a few rows an' just go off an' let no one know where he's at!"

"No, it don't," replied Jim. "Still, he must have ridden off with his team and wagon of his own accord. I recall Montgomery telling us before the Race that he hid out a spell once in No Man's Land when the revenuers were after him and his partner for rum running. But you'd think they'd leave a man alone that's trying to prove up a claim! Wouldn't you think so, Hank?"

"Sure would!" Hank exclaimed and added, "Hope he ain't in no trouble that's keepin' him away."

"Hope you're right, Hank," Jim said. "Course all that other happened in Indian Territory before Charley Montgomery got shot in cold blood by Bob Dalton and by one of his lookouts. Josh took that awful hard, the way he told it. Said his half-brother was all he had in the world. Reckon Josh don't exactly need to be on his claim more than a few months a year if the work the government expects from us is done. Josh knows that. Shucks Hank! Here we are worrying about Josh when that ole buzzard can take care of himself without us. I'll bet on that."

"But, Jim, I'm concerned anyway."

"Well, I'll admit something did occur to me, but it is unlikely to be of any consequence." Jim paused, then continued with his thought. "You know Charley Montgomery was buried over in Coffeyville. Some kind of twisted fate caused his murderers to be buried in the same cemetery a few years afterwards, like vengeance took a hand in it. You heard the story about the outraged citizens of Coffeyville taking matters in their own hands when the Daltons tried to rob two banks there at the same time? It was a shoot-out to the death. They got the Dalton outlaws and only Emmet, the youngest, lived and he was shot to pieces. Guess there was a dozen people killed within the space of a few minutes. Boot Hill was a pretty busy place for the next few days."

"Do you think Josh was mixed up in that?" Hank asked.

"That was all over and done, so I can't figure how Josh could have a hand in anything like that now, could you, Hank? It isn't like this renegade, Dick Yeager, who lived right here in Oklahoma Territory out by Boggy Creek near Enid that the three posses were after. Yet Yeager outwitted his pursuers time after time because some of the people were in sympathy with him. He was wounded time and again. It's said folks hid him. But a feller doesn't get it 'til his number's up! Then all hell can't stop it! He died in prison. The doc said why fix up his wounds just to get him hanged anyway. That surely was something," Jim concluded and shook his head.

Jim was all wound up when the subject of desperadoes was mentioned. He had kept his suspicions to himself so long that he found it a source of relief to talk around them even if he dared not go deeper into what he really suspected. He wondered who had been Bob Dalton's lookout on the night of Charley's murder. He also wondered if the lookout was with the Daltons at the Coffeyville shoot-out. Time would turn up some clues. Time had a way of doing that. Better to wait and see, Jim told himself as he finished his reverie.

Some weeks went by, and one day when Jim passed the Montgomery claim he saw fresh wagon tracks. He took time to go up to the house and take a look around. There was still no life on the place, but through a knothole Jim saw some crates stacked one on top of the other, two to a row.

"By jiminy, so this has become a storehouse for something without any labels!" Then he said to himself, "what's wrong with me? If it's ole red eye, what of it? Hooch is legal here in Oklahoma Territory. Montgomery couldn't go to the hoosegow for that. But, if he takes a notion to tote it over to Indian Territory, then it's a federal offense!"

Several weeks later when Jim was again passing Josh's claim, he saw a team tethered out front. He turned in expecting to see Josh and have a showdown with him. To his surprise, a much younger man confronted him. The newcomer identified himself as a friend of Josh Montgomery.

"I was lookin' for Montgomery," Jim explained.

"Josh told me 'bout his friends around here. Let's see, you must be Crouch?" the stranger stated. "Bout forty, ain't you?"

"Sure feel forty, but I'm not that old," Jim replied. "You're right, I'm him, but who are you?"

The stranger smiled and took a sheet of legal-sized paper out of his pocket and handed it to Jim to read, saying at the same time, "I'm Frank Coffee."

Jim scanned the page, which read:

> *To whom this may concern:*
> *The bearer of this note, Frank Coffee, is authorized to take over my claim and work it until further notice, or until I return.*

Josh Montgomery had signed the document, though obviously hadn't written it.

"Did he write this in your presence?" Jim inquired carefully.

"Well, it's his signature, ain't it?" Coffee replied.

"I see you've already plowed a few rows for Josh. Hank and I were getting mighty concerned about Josh's absence. We were afraid he'd lose his claim," Jim told him, adding, "suppose he'll be coming along right soon?"

Coffee was noncommittal and shrugged as if in doubt.

As Crouch was leaving, he gave Coffee a message for Josh.

"Tell Josh when you see him that I have some business with him that I want to straighten out."

Jim noticed that the crates were missing but he was not supposed to know about them, so he asked no questions, considering it was none of his business.

Jim felt convinced that Frank Coffee was not a ruthless claim-jumper, yet had certain reservations regarding some shady transactions between him and Josh. He decided to await further developments. Three months later, in June, Jim noticed that the newcomer had really worked the claim sufficiently to satisfy government requirements. Since the Race, the claimants had only one year left of the five in which to prove up their claims. Time had flown since the evening on which he and Hank, riding double on Barney, had trailed into Alva to join the line and register their hard-won claims.

PHOTOGRAPHS

Oklahoma Panhandle, 1888
Drovers by the chuck wagon taking an extra hour at noon. Jim Crouch is
at upper right.

James (Jim) Crouch, II

Elizabeth (Lizzie) Bevis Crouch

Alvin Bevis on horse, Ott Bevis, Freddy Crouch, Lizzie Crouch holding
Mabel, Gladys Crouch, Robbie Crouch, Grandfather Levi Bevis, Opal
Bevis, Charley Bevis, Grandmother Alma Bevis.

The Sod House 1898
Over Prairie grass today I trod on virgin sod--- where no
Man of mortal coil---ever put plowshares to the soil---of
The Cherokee Nation. Where grew no trees for logs; or rocks
To shelter man or flocks, --so I cut the turf into a thou-
sand blocks—and made a sod-house habitation.

Gladys Crouch Clark 1975

Lizzie and Jim Crouch.

Gladys, at age 4, and Mabel, at age 2.

Gladys Crouch at age 12.

Gladys Crouch in 1909, at age 13.

Gladys Crouch, 1910 at age 14.

Gladys Crouch, 1912, at age 16.

Gladys Crouch, 1914, with a cousin on the left, and youngest sister, Esselgeane at age 2.

Gladys Crouch Clark in December, 1915, after August marriage to
Charles Clark.

Gladys Crouch Clark 1916.

Gladys Crouch Clark with sister Esselgeane Alva, OK, 1917

Gladys C. Clark with brother Jack, age 3, and sister Esselgeane, age 5,
Alva, OK, 1917

The Gable House, Alva, OK, 1912

Bevis family at funeral of grandfather Levi W. Bevis, October 1913,
Alva, OK
Sons: Charles Bevis, Alvin Bevis, Levi Bevis, and Ott Bevis.
Daughters: Vena Coombs, Elizabeth Crouch, and Opal Menefee.
Wife: Alma Tower Bevis

Lizzie Crouch in 1935, in front of the Gable House, Alva, OK

The Crouch family at the funeral of their mother Lizzie Bevis Crouch,
Santa Barbara, CA 1949.
From left: Robert Crouch, Gladys Clark, Maybelle (Mabel) Hinkey,
Grace Stauffer, Joe Crouch, Frank Crouch, Esselgeane McKellar, and
Jack Crouch.

CHAPTER 13

LIZZIE'S SADNESS

The stormy weather eased up after Easter of 1898, and about this time Lizzie found herself in the midst of ongoing activity. The plans for the new house were drawn and redrawn. Lizzie and Jim had already chosen the site, but the foundation plans were the center of lively discussion between the men. Jim, Pa Bevis, Hank and Ott would measure distances and take into the consideration the merits and drawbacks of the types of materials available.

The seasonal farming activities gathered momentum as new animals were born and others were bought, sold or traded. Lizzie's garden was behind schedule because she was slower to regain her energy following Mabel's birth in March of 1898. She attributed her lack of strength not to the new baby, but to the constant care, day and night, which little Freddy required.

Lizzie was no less cheerful than usual but in the midst of everything she was entering a retrospective period, mentally drawing breath. In later years she would recall the time from about June 1897 until the spring of 1899 as a separate time.

She seemed to function somewhat separate from her ongoing daily activities. Always, there was a niggling doubt somewhere at the back of her consciousness that Freddy was not growing into a healthy child like his brother and sisters. Her journal reflected some of the recurring dynamics.

Excerpts from Lizzie's Journal

June, 1897. Jim still hasn't heard anything from Josh. He went by the place again today when he was in town, and there was no sign of Frank Coffee either. But the place was well tended, so I suppose everything is all right. Jim picked up the reaper part and my catalogue order at the railroad depot.

I ordered yard goods and yarn. I will need to make new fall clothes for the children and I want to knit for the new baby who will be coming in the spring of '98. Guess having babies does get easier as Ma says! I've had no morning sickness with this one, thank the Lord. It's a good thing! There have been so many rest-broken nights with little Freddy, I'm glad that I don't feel ill.

The mornings are quite cool, and Freddy coughs a lot, despite the stove. I keep it banked to warm him until the sun is high. It's hot for the others, but he is always so cold. Still, the other children run out early to be with Ott, getting the horses yoked up, and the chickens fed.

It will be wonderful when we have our new frame home built. It is pleasant enough to be able to do the washing outdoors and look at the creek and the birds when I go to my garden. But it will be so good to come indoors to a real house after the dugout and Pa's sod house.

August, 1897. When the harvesters left to move up North we did not have to cook so much. The last few weeks I've been busy canning vegetables and fruit. I've hardly had time to stop and think, and Freddy has kept me up so many nights.

September, 1897. We spent most of the day taking in the dried herbs and tying them in bunches. The sage and thyme will be good with the Thanksgiving turkey. I finally reared six turkeys from a setting of eggs from Mrs. McCullough in Alva. I gave her a set of crocheted mats in return. She told me she has had many compliments on them. Those turkey chicks gave me fits, but the six I raised look real good. Guess chopping those collard greens gave them the iron they needed. I must sew a new smock for church. Soon I won't feel like being around too many social gatherings, the way I look and all.

November, 1897. The men spent most of last month clearing the fields and preparing for the winter wheat. Funny how men tidy-up in the fall, while we women seem to do it in the spring. Got some antelope last week, we roasted some and Ma made her red currant jelly and the combination was mighty good. It's an old recipe from way back:

Wash 3 cups currants in clear water. Add 1 cup sugar, a squeeze of lemon, if you have it, or a teaspoon of apple juice or vinegar. Add a half-teaspoon of mixed spices, and 1 cup boiling water. Bring it all to a simmer, put the lid on the pot and when the scum rises to the top it is done. Skim it, serve it or can it.

We made jerky with the rest of the antelope meat. The men enjoy it when they are out working and Freddy likes to chew on a little now and then.

Thanksgiving was a break. We all sat down to dinner and Pa carved one of our own turkeys. We have much to be thankful for.

December, 1897. The baby is becoming active and I have most of the baby things made so we are ready when he or she arrives. We would love another son, but we'll welcome whatever the Lord sends.

Jim gave me a little gold watch brooch that I can wear on my dress. I love it. It's beautiful. I suspect he got it from the mail order catalog. I made Jim a pair of deerskin gloves to keep warm, and help his poor hand from getting stiff. It was tricky to make that right hand glove with the special finger in it. Ott made us a nice iron trivet for hot pots. That boy is getting to be real handy working with iron. Some day he'll be a good blacksmith. I made doll clothes for Gladys, a wool cap from scraps for Rob, a little jacket for Freddy and a lot of cookies and candy.

Christmas was quiet and we stayed home. We hung up the children's socks at the ends of their beds.

Late on New Year's Eve, after the children were asleep, Jim handed me my shawl and asked me to come out for a minute. We walked for a little while. There was a hard frost over everything and the sky was clear and sprinkled with stars. We stood in the icy cold and looked over the vast silent stretches of the prairie and Jim had his arms around me. I thought of the struggle we had had, and the year that lay ahead, the child we'd soon have, the one that lay sleeping uneasily inside, and the other two playful as lambs, and the house we would build. We turned our backs on the Old Year and silently faced the year ahead with hope. Jim took my hand and we went indoors to bed. And so we begin another year.

February, 1898. It would seem that the world has been asleep for a month. Now, I feel as if my time is near and I long to hold the new baby in my arms.

March, 1898. My second daughter, Mabel arrived on that first day of March, with comparative ease for all concerned. Ma took care of me, and Ellie took care of Rob, Gladys and Freddy. Jim is delighted.

***

A great deal had taken place at the Crouch homestead despite the handicap of the injury to Jim's right hand. The finger had healed crookedly with permanent rigidity from the knuckle to the fingertip. The condition prevented any firm grip of tools, and he had little maneuverability in his hand to back up heavy ranch chores. Jim had not realized how much he needed to rely on and utilize his left hand.

The frame house under construction would be one of the most modern for the time and for the area. Lizzie and Jim had talked long hours over the plans before they sought opinions from any of their relatives and friends. They had held off the actual work as long as possible. Every mail packet from back east brought periodicals with new ideas and materials.

The children required constant attention. By tacit understanding they did not discuss Freddy's health except when Lizzie looked particularly weary after spending a night without rest tending to him. He was not a fretful child. He was so quiet and always smiling, but he never showed any improvement. Jim was a little disappointed not to have more sons, since Freddy seemed to be puny without hope of developing enough for farm work, and Robbie was what the schoolmarm called precocious. Robbie, with a little help from everyone around, could read from his ABC book, and write and figure a little before he was four years of age. He could make his father's fiddle sound like music, and he could draw adult-looking pictures. Lizzie was convinced that he should get the opportunity to pursue these talents, not reckoning that he first needed discipline. Lizzie preferred his artistic talents and did not encourage Robbie to develop physical prowess.

"Virgin soil! Ribbons of sod cut up in blocks! That is what we are living in, cold and dreary, chilling to the bone." Lizzie complained to herself. She felt the need of warmth, so after the children were tucked in she sought comfort in wool blankets wondering if their dream house would ever get built. She was ashamed of her brief moment of doubt and pessimism. Her strength of spirit had always been unshakable.

After a short and disturbed sleep Lizzie awoke with instant foreboding. She listened. What was that rasping sound? Jim was asleep at her side and needed his rest so she would see to it herself.

She threw the wool shawl around her shoulders, pushing her toes into soft carpet slippers. The children were recovering from the measles but little amiable Freddy had had considerable fever. Expecting gradual recovery she made her way to their beds and found Freddy's brow hot with fever. As she picked him up in her arms the wall clock struck twelve in long cadences as if it needed winding. Sitting in the rocker by the stove, with her come-see child on her lap, she rocked him back and forth. Lizzie shivered as her intuition prepared her to give up her second-born child.

How very frail and weak his body felt and his breathing labored. Lizzie's anguish had to be borne alone for the moment at least, until she could get a grip on herself. She kept on rocking in a rhythm of soothing movements when suddenly a warmth and peace came to her mind like a beneficent presence.

In a trance-like doze Lizzie saw dimly a procession of angelic troops cross the Plains before her. It seemed that they were carrying in their arms souls of little ones, embodied like her own, clasped with loving care. One shining angel broke ranks and came toward her, tenderly lifted up her precious child in enfolding arms, saying "We are the Troops of Eternity claiming our own." Suddenly awakened from her dream Lizzie felt the cool brow and knew at once that her little boy had departed this world.

At last she returned the lifeless form to the trundle bed. Now her concern was how to break the news to Jim without breaking herself. Lizzie first went to Mabel's crib. Finding her sleeping well and free of fever Lizzie walked over to the corner of the room draped off with calico curtains. Gladys was awake and wondering why the lamp was turned up and what was going on. Lizzie pulled up a stool and sat down beside her, resting her head on the pillow next to her. The words came: "Little Freddy just died and somehow I must go and tell Papa now."

CHAPTER 14

THE CIRCUS

No matter how well prepared a family is for a loved one's passing, when the sad event occurs, the shock is as great as if there had been no warning of any kind.

And so it was with the Crouch and Bevis families for a long while after little Freddy died. Life went on, but the fair spring weather and the resurgence of prairie life did little to lift the unspoken sadness which hung about the farm and the family like a damp dark curtain, keeping the light and laughter from doing more than peeping through the folds of the fabric.

Another event set a milestone in time. Only from then on, and from that event did their lives begin to move forward. The family, old and young, large and small, began to smile and live again as if all had been granted a collective reprieve from grief and sadness.

Late that summer of 1899 Robbie came home from a school outing fairly bursting with excitement, but he waited until the evening meal to tell the family there was a man in funny-looking clothes who was nailing up posters all over town. Another strangely dressed man was passing out handbills to the towns-people on the street. In response to questions, Robbie produced and put on the table several handbills he had brought from town advertising that a circus was coming to Alva in two weeks.

Robbie looked from one to the other of his parents a little nervously, but he smiled his sweetest smile and tried to chase the habitual mischievous look out of the corners of his eyes. His parents exchanged glances. Lizzie's lip quivered a little, but Jim reached across the table and took her hand and held it.

"What do you think, Jamie?" Lizzie asked Jim haltingly.

"Why not, Lizzie?" he answered. "The circus doesn't usually come this way and I think we're due for a completely free day, or as I should have said, a day free of care. There's nothing free about an outing like this. But that's all right, right now. What d'you think?"

"Yes," she said with a little smile. "Let's go. And let's enjoy every minute of it!"

For days the excited children asked questions concerning the circus. "What is a circus? What do the circus people do? Why do they dress so funny? Are those REAL animals?" Jim and Lizzie answered the children the best they could but finally told them to wait and see.

Several advance circus personnel arrived in Alva to announce to the townspeople that the Forepaugh Circus would be coming to their town in two weeks. They passed out gaily decorated handbills to all the townspeople they met and placed them in all the store windows and shops they could so everyone would be sure to see them.

The big day finally came. After breakfast and the morning chores were finished, Jim piled the impatient children in the back of the buckboard along with the blankets and picnic baskets Lizzie had prepared. They all headed to town to join the rest of the family members and friends to watch the exciting and colorful circus parade march down the main street of Alva. When they reached town, Jim drove behind the main hotel and tied the horses to the hitching post in back. He joined the rest of their group on the second floor balcony to watch the parade pass by.

They heard a drum roll and then a trumpet blared at the far end of the main street. "Here they come!" Robbie hollered, jumping up and down.

First came two elaborately dressed horsemen, holding high the circus banner between them. Behind them, eight dappled gray horses pulled a large brightly painted wagon, which carried the circus band playing their tunes. Then the tumblers and acrobats marched by showing off their stunts every few yards. A circus lady was next, dressed in a pink tutu and tights with silver slippers and a cape. She rode on a snow-white steed, outfitted in a pink and silver braided bridle and pink blanket.

The crowd oohed and aahed and clapped their hands as two elephants preceded the lions and tigers in their red and gold rolling cages. A calliope followed on another red and gold wagon. Jim suggested that the familiar music kept the big cats calm in a strange place.

Gladys thought for a moment and said, "Papa, aren't strange places home to these traveling animals? Won't they be at home everywhere?"

"Honey, you have a point." Jim said. "However, circus people and their animals do have an off-season when they stay in one place for about four or five months. I read an article somewhere that tells about an eastern circus called Ringling that sets up permanent homes for the circus folks for when they are not on the road traveling from place to place."

The child smiled without further comment as if she were sharing a secret with herself. The movements of her family recaptured her attention as they repaired to the hotel lobby before traveling with other friends to the circus grounds.

Robbie's eyes grew large as saucers as he saw the flags and bunting and the balloons flying about the perimeter of the circus. The scene was indeed like a small village. Jim took them along the arcade and pointed out the different side shows along the way, but when they exhibited curiosity at the peep and girlie show, he took Lizzie's arm and Gladys's hand and quickly led them away. "That peep show is not for little girls, or big ones either," he said firmly.

Robbie and Gladys each won prizes on the coconut shy[1]. Then Jim won a couple of toys at the shooting gallery, so Mabel would be having a surprise when the family returned for her at her grandmother's home.

The making of the spun sugar into cotton candy fascinated the children and they had their first glimpse of how corn was popped by a machine. Thus fortified by these new treats, the Crouch party sat on the tiered benches. Not long after, Hank and Ellie and their little ones joined them.

The canvas flaps swayed in the gentle breeze, the sawdust of the ring gave off its special odor, and the band tuned their instruments. Experimental blasts on a trumpet made everyone seated inside jump. When every seat and bench was filled, the gold silken ropes drew back the blue velvet curtains at one end of the arena and the Ringmaster walked straight into the ring.

---

1 Sidestall game where a player using wooden balls attempts to hit coconuts balanced on posts.

"Lai-dees a-n-d Gentle-men! It gives me great pleasure to present for your enjoy-ment:

THE WORLD RENOWNED FOREPAUGHS CIR-CUS!"

And the show was on. He ran out of the ring, narrowly missed by three bustling elephants coming in, trunk to tail, as if they barely had time to do their act. There were acrobats, tight-rope walkers, fire eaters, a sword-swallower, big cats, small cats, a dog act and trick riders, trick-shooting cowboys and cowgirls, and a frightening knife-thrower who narrowly missed chopping the bow off his lady's hair. A man appeared who seemed to actually chop a brave spectator in two inside a box. But Jim said it was all make-believe. Who knew, who cared? On that day everyone was taken into a different world, and away from daily chores. There was so much that was new, so many unexpected things, that there were times when Lizzie laughed so hard that she cried. Jim held her hand. The children stared and smiled and clapped, but only after they had grown accustomed to the strange sights.

The clowns held the whole show together. Aware of their audience, they broke moments of tension without detracting from the performers in center ring. They were in and out of the audience, jumping on passing horses, leaping off seesaws, and running to the side of any mother who had a frightened or a tearful child.

When the finale came, the children were immersed in a collage of color, fabric, sound, animals, people, and at center ring, the Ringmaster. For the second time that afternoon he removed his glossy top hat and swept it to his knees, bowing to the audience.

"Good people of Alva, I thank you from the bottom of my heart. You have given us a royal welcome, and you have taken us to your hearts, we thank you one and all." Again bowing deeply he repeated "Ladies and Gentlemen" as he left the circus ring.

Jim took everyone back to the hotel, and then went to fetch the buckboard. Ellie and Lizzie chatted and the children compared notes. They made a lazy journey homeward in the setting sun while the plots for many stories were woven in sleepy heads.

Jim held the reins in one hand and fingered his pipe with the other hand. Lizzie smiled as she talked to him, the kind of smile that he had not seen for a very long time.

CHAPTER 15

THE NEW LIFE

"I'm in the family way again," Lizzie told Ellie, "but this time we'll have the home I've always dreamed about. We'll have plenty of room for this little one that arrives next June." Ellie confided that she, too, was expecting in the late summer of 1900. The Hartners had two boys and Ellie was hoping for a little girl.

According to custom, the newly built frame home was painted white. It stood sparkling in the crisp spring sunlight. Jim and Lizzie had purchased much of the furniture in Alva, and ordered many items from the catalogue. Her pride and joy was an upholstered horsehair couch with a curved, dark walnut frame. The Axminster carpet had a floral design in bright colors. Lizzie had bought an organ of black walnut with stops and foot pedals that pumped. The dining room table was oblong in shining golden oak with chairs to match. The golden oak sideboard had claw feet to match the table legs. The black walnut bedroom pieces included a bureau with marble slabs on the raised side drawer tops and in the lower section in between. Short, top-like posters stood at attention at the corners of the bedstead made of flat black walnut sides.

A large kitchen cupboard held dishes, glassware, pots, pans and other cooking utensils. The kitchen table had a tin flour bin underneath that pulled out on one side. The other side had three drawers for cutlery. Jim had paid $26.50 for the Acme Sterling Steel Range that burned both coal or wood.

The house gained in elegance and individuality when Jim bought tall spires of shiny metal to put on the ridge of the roof. These were really something new. The salesman called them lightening rods.

"A home isn't safe at all, especially when there are little ones to protect," he assured the Crouches.

"But just exactly how do lightning rods keep thunder 'n lightning off the house?" Lizzie asked.

"They are grounded at the lower end and keep the lightning away from the structure," the salesman replied. "A sort of conductor it is."

"I know it's way beyond my imagination," Lizzie said. "But with these fierce storms, if anything will keep lightning from striking this house and setting it afire, Jim an' me want it even if we cain't afford it."

Jim was still unconvinced, and this expenditure would call for cash that he did not consider his to spend. But fearing that Lizzie would think that the children did not come first in his considerations, Jim paid for the lightning rods the day they were installed, partly with money that he owed Josh. Despite his mild growls about slick-talking dudes a-turning folks heads, he was pleased with the decorative effect of the rods and added his hopes that they would be as functionally efficient as they were handsome in appearance.

The coming harvest was two months away yet, but after selling his wheat crop Jim expected to keep more surplus funds. Josh was now almost a memory. Lizzie took the extra hens' eggs and butter to the general store in Alva. She traded her fresh dairy products for credit towards the purchase of goods shipped out from the East. In this near-barter system, goodwill was so important to both seller and buyer that the notion of interest or service charges didn't occur to them. It was a simple community of neighbors doing business in a manner where each was conscious of the convenience of the other.

Lizzie did not want to be conspicuous in pregnancy so she put up a supply of salted cod in wooden buckets, nourishment that would keep during the period when she would not be going out in the community. Nellie gave bountifully of milk, so there was a plentiful supply for oyster stew made with canned oysters. Her family warmly received this change of pace at the supper table. Lizzie soaked the salt cod overnight, flaking the drained fish in the morning. She made delectable fish cakes by mixing the flaked fish with mashed potatoes, pepper, salt, and a little milk or an egg to bind the mixture. Next, she dipped the fish cakes or fish balls in batter and fried them quickly in hot lard to a golden brown on the outside while keeping the inside white and tender. Occasionally during the harvest season, she served up codfish balls to the threshing crew at breakfast along with sowbelly bacon, eggs, sausages, biscuits and coffee. No place else on the Strip had as popular a kitchen as Lizzie. She kept the best table around that part of the country.

A milk shed containing a cistern was attached to the kitchen. She kept jars of milk and crocks of butter and cream on shelves there. Lizzie's brother Charley had made custom shelves exactly to her specifications. After she finished churning, the buttermilk left from the separation of cream into butter was usually poured into the swill pails which were left outside near the rain barrel. Regular buttermilk drinkers only wanted it fresh-churned and preferably cold. Lizzie had her tricks for cooling it because ice was rarely available to her. All of her tin buckets she accumulated from sorghum and some wooden buckets left from apple butter or codfish, she scalded with boiling water and salt. Later she filled these with milk, cream, buttermilk, or butter, and tied cords to each handle, and then lowered them into the cool cistern. The butter came up semi-hard and the buttermilk, after a few hours there, was a delightful cool drink with bits of butter swimming on the top.

The Bevis clan kept busy with their chores and projects. Pa Bevis built the chairs and rockers used by the family. He trimmed worn leather harness strips unfit for further use as gear and stained them with black walnut shells. He then cut the strips in desired lengths and cross-wove them into seats on hand-made walnut frames. The Bevis boys took turns currying the horses, cleaning stalls, feeding, and generally keeping up with the yard and buildings. One of the boys would bring the cows in at milking time, and give them a few ears of corn to keep them occupied while milking was in progress. A cow could not be left loose in a corral with horses, lest an 'ornery' or a playful horse kicked the living daylights out of her. A good cow was a pampered animal, worth her weight in returns. She deserved her own sleeping quarters, grazing area and water, and she usually got it.

In most farm kitchens, schmerkase, as cottage cheese was called, was a popular item. The women set the milk on the back of the stove at very low heat for several hours. The resulting steeped clabber was put into a clean cheesecloth bag to drain. They served the curd with a little cream and a pinch of salt, the whey skimmed off to add to the swill pail for the hogs.

***

Baby Grace took her first peek at the world on the summer solstice, June 21, 1900 on a lovely calm day. The wheat had been threshed and the harvesters were ready to leave after their noon meal on the child's day of birth. Ordinarily, Jim would have taken the first load of wheat to the granary in town, but he was overjoyed with the new infant. He felt he was needed to help Ma Bevis and Ellie, who had come over to help out. This time Lizzie had made arrangements with a mid-wife to attend her. Ma Bevis was left free to help with the extra cooking for the harvest hands. Of course Lizzie and Jim had one brief moment of disappointment that the new baby was not a boy, but they knew that what the Lord sent was what He intended.

CHAPTER 16

ON THE LAM

That evening the wind rose, blowing up a hot, dry dust storm. While Jim was still in the kitchen closing up the windows, he heard a voice calling from the outside. The harvesters[1] had left at noon and he thought one of them had returned for some gear he might have left, and he went to the door to let him in.

He stepped back in astonishment when he saw who it was.

"Josh, y'ole sidewinder!" Jim said with a welcoming grin. "Where have you been all this time? Hank and me have been worried that something wrong had happened to you! Come in and sit down and tell me what you've been up to."

Josh put his finger to his lips and said, "Can we be alone in here without anybody hearin' us talk?"

"Sure, Josh. Lizzie's resting in bed and her Ma's putting the little ones to sleep and no one else is around."

Sitting opposite each other at the table, Josh leaned towards Jim and spoke in a low voice.

"Jim, I'm goin' to need your help. Kin 'ya let me have some of my money back tonight? I've got to hide out for a bit."

"What's your hurry, Josh?" Jim questioned. "Can't you wait till tomorrow and then I can pay you all of it? I kept the money I owed you right here, used the first hundred, but when that lightning rod dude came along I had to use the rest. Who's after you, Josh, some of them outlaws that you might have had a run-in with?"

Jim hesitated a moment, then he looked directly at his friend and added, "Josh, I might as well let you understand that I've knowed all along who stabbed that braggart outside the saloon the day after the Strip opened. Why did you do it, man? That money you loaned me was taken from his pocket, wasn't it?"

---

1 At this latitude wheat ripens at the end of May, but the temporary harvest help work until mid-July.

Josh sighed, slowly nodding his head, "Jim, you don't understand. That villain was Sim Sharkey, the lookout for Bob Dalton, who was just as guilty as Dalton in my brother's murder. Charley didn't get a chance to defend himself. He was not a culprit. He didn't want no trouble! Just returned to get his clothes and gear from the horse barn where he had bin working, and the dastardly, trigger-happy butchers gunned him down in cold blood. Bob Dalton got his end over in Coffeyville but Sim Sharkey was roamin' free, an' robbin' trains with the tag-end of the gang. He helped to kill the only livin' family I had and robbed me of all hope of us gettin' a big stake together. So what I took from him was a little down-payment on what I was denied."

"But how did you recognize him?" Jim asked "And if he was with the outlaws that robbed the train at Red Rock, why didn't you let the law handle it?"

"I seen Sim Sharkey once at Guthrie, and knew his connection with the Daltons before they turned desperado. All I had to do was to find out from the folks around the stable where Charley worked, who Bob Dalton's lookout was the night of the murder."

Josh looked around the room. Jim saw him relax and let him continue.

"It took a long while," Josh said, "but I checked it out three ways, and the name turned out to be Sim Sharkey, all three times. I knew his name before the Race, and I swore vengeance as soon as I found out who done it, although Charley had been dead for several years. I took time off to make the Race and get my claim started, and a lucky fate brought the murderin' scalawag right to me. I did what I had to do, an' took nothin' that warn't comin' to me! The lawmen had all the time they needed to catch the train robbers. Everyone thought they was part of the Dalton gang, but they failed to get the evidence."

"Josh, there's some questions that come to my mind," said Jim inquiringly. "Who was the dark stranger that took Sim Sharkey to the Kansas border the night of the storm, after the stabbing? And what was his connection with the whole affair?"

"He was one of the gang that rode with Sim, one of the train robbers, I guess. He prob'ly was goin' to meet Sim at the tent saloon when that thunderstorm blew up, and they each thought of gettin' out afore it broke. The feller's name is Gambell, as near as I could make out, but he sure knows who I am. He's been on my trail for months."

Again Josh stopped, reflecting before continuing with the story. Jim sat quietly, waiting.

"Course I was safe in the jug for the first offense of rum-runnin' for awhile in the old Chickasaw Nation near Tishomino," Josh said. "I done my stretch, but that crazy galoot scented out my trail and I've been on the lam from him ever since." The timbre of his voice assumed a mournful quality. "It's goin' to be a show-down betwixt him 'n me afore long and my eyes cain't pick out the target like they used to. That's why I gotta git goin' fast."

Jim had already turned down the lamp and now he turned the wick lower, until neither man's features would be recognizable in the dim light. He spoke to Josh in a soft voice.

"Tell me," Jim said. "Did you ever find out Sharkey's fate, is he dead or alive? I'd like to know too, why a man of property like yourself would go back to rum-running?"

"Jim, ya' still don't understand. I told ya when Charley was done in I swore vengeance. He woulda done the same for me. I don't rightly know if Sharkey is alive or dead but I do know he came to long enough to put the finger on me. Rum runnin', the way Charley and me figured, was nobody's business as long as we didn't sell nonc to no Injuns that cain't handle it. But white men ought to get liquor when they need it, for medicine or for courage. You know that, Jim. Besides, I was helpin' out a friend. We got across the Territory border from Texas with a sizable load and thought it was safe."

Josh smiled here, obviously more relaxed since he had begun to sense Jim's understanding, if not his agreement. "My partner went to sleep in the back of the wagon," Josh said, "and I was up front, drivin' the team. I'da got a stiffer term, but all the marshal took out was one bottle. While he was hand-cuffin' me, my partner snuck up under the seat, grabbed the reins, took off, an' got away with the rest of the evidence. He made it all the way to Oklahoma Territory where rum is legal."

"You talking about Frank Coffee?" Jim asked. "Then you did send him to do the work necessary to prove up your claim? When did you make the agreement betwixt you all?"

"Well, Jim, I ain't on no witness stand," Josh replied. "But if ya want to know, it was made afore we went over the Texas border to get the rum just in case we got into any trouble with the law, either of us. He gave me a similar letter. Coffee's got forty acres of land already patented near El Reno. We ain't got nobody but ourselves to belong to." Josh lamented.

"Coffee has been plowing and planting some," Jim said. "I hope he can satisfy the government's conditions. I already got my claim proved up. Come to think of it Josh, when did you see Frank Coffee after you got clinked?"

"You surely are nosy, Jim! Actin' like a lawyer. Frank came to see me in the hoosegow. An important thing happened after that. See, when I got jugged, this circuit judge had just been around and left and wasn't expected back for four or five months. I was restless as a skunk on a beehive, wantin' my case to be heard. I cussed my dastardly luck. But by the time the judge got around the circuit again, they couldn't find all the evidence. Oh, the bottle was there all right with my name tagged on it, but someone had done in the contents! Then my case was dismissed for lack evidence. Good fortune was smilin' my way at last, I thought." Josh hesitated for a moment.

"Guess it wasn't long before this Gambell got hep to where you was, Josh," Jim commented. "Who would have tipped him off? Who would benefit if someone got you out of the way and knows about the stabbing of Sim Sharkey?" He asked Josh.

Josh hesitated for a moment, then said, "Why, only you, Jim, that I know of. You're the only one that would benefit. You wouldn't need to pay me back the loan. I never told nobody. Not a soul!"

"Well, look where my line of questioning has put me," Jim grumbled. "Now I become the stool-pidgin suspect. I never used but one hundred of your tainted money until that slick lightning rod salesman come along, and then I used the rest of it. My family is increasing by leaps and bounds, and I wanted the family safe. The last infant, born today, is a girl. Three girls in a row!"

Jim could have kicked himself for allowing matters to put him in such an awkward hole. He found that sparring for his honor was distasteful.

"Josh, I'll give you fifty dollars tonight," he said. "Tomorrow night, I'll give you the other hundred and fifty, plus interest. But you'll have to stay over at Hank's. There's too many folks running in and out of here, and somebody is apt to see you. I'll get that grain to town first thing in the morning, unless this wind storm picks it all up and blows it away."

"Why Jim," Josh said, "I didn't mean for a minute that I thought ya tipped Gambell off about me, but it was the way ya put it, askin' who would benefit. Now I see I've got to give it some sober thought. Come on, take me over to Hank's place. You go in and explain first. Tell him I'll be on my way after twenty-four hours."

"Josh, do yourself a favor. If you haven't already seen Coffee this trip, don't do it. That's all I got to say." Jim hesitated, and then added, "I've taken your word, Josh, that you are clean with the law. Couldn't let the Hartners harbor someone that was wanted. But it's darn good to see you and Hank will be glad to have you there."

Later that night, after Jim returned from Hank's place, he thought about his conversation with Josh. The whole affair was pretty much what he had figured it to be. Despite everything, Jim hoped Josh would soon come home to stay, but realized that there still remained unfinished business for Josh and some unknown person.

CHAPTER 17

CHARLIE'S WEDDING

Jim would long remember the busy day of June 22, 1900. When he returned from selling his load of wheat in town and doing the farm chores, he hurried to take his weekly bath in the tin washtub. His presence at Charlie Bevis' wedding was expected and he didn't want to be late. Lizzie was lying in with the newborn, vicariously enjoying all the excitement, but there was no way that she could attend the festivities. The Reverend Perkins and his good lady, Linda, would remain as overnight guests at the Crouch claim as the Bevis boys were planning a shivaree[1] for their brother and his bride. Linda Perkins had remarked earlier that she found excessive noise uncomfortable so it suited her purposes very well to be able to stay with Lizzie and help to look after the younger children. It would also present an opportunity for the two women to visit and catch up on their news. The Perkins always enjoyed a visit with the Crouches and the Reverend was fond of confiding to his wife that he wished that more of his flock had the pleasant and upstanding characteristics of the young couple. He always remembered to request in his prayers more sons to help Jim, whenever he learned in a round-about way that Lizzie was in the family way. In contrast to his wife, Reverend Perkins enjoyed officiating at weddings and participating in all of the pranks and revelry as long as a modicum of decorum prevailed.

While Lizzie was having her supper in bed, Jim saddled Barney, who was still strong and frisky despite his added years, and rode over to Hartner's place where Josh was staying. He only stayed long enough to pay Josh the balance of the principal and the interest due on the loan. Jim felt relief and freedom at the conclusion of the transaction.

In Hank's presence Jim said, "Josh, this ends our transaction. We are even now." Jim added, "No hard feelings Josh, and I surely

---

1 North American term for a clamorous salutation made to a newlywed couple by an assembled crowd of neighbors and friends, often conducted in the middle of the night, accompanied by banging on pots and pans and other noisemakers.

do thank you for helping me and giving me the use of the money. I only wish that you'd get back to your land and be a citizen and neighbor among us. We'd all welcome you back. You got your vengeance, and see what it's getting you? Hiding out from a man sworn to kill you for getting one of his gang, and who makes your future seem mighty slim."

"Good luck, Josh," Jim said. They shook hands, and Jim mounted Barney and headed for Charlie's wedding.

Jim approached the Bevis sod house, grateful to be on a horse so that he didn't have to find a place to park among the throng of buggies and buckboards crowded about the place. The other invited guests had arrived, welcomed by all kinds of noise that Levi, Jr., and Alvin, busy as chickadees feeding nestlings, thought up for the shivaree until Alma sent Pa Bevis out to put a stop to the premature celebration.

Finally, the wedding party drove up. The bride and her retinue, composed of her father and sister Jane, had traveled the thirty miles from Waynoka to Alva by train. Ott Bevis, the best man, had taken his dad's new rig and his fast half-Morgan, half-thoroughbred sorrel sprinter to Alva to meet the wedding party. The bride and her sister hurried inside and changed into their wedding finery. When she was ready, her father escorted her towards the beaming groom.

While the wedding ceremony was in progress, Ellie Hartner glanced around at the women and admired the fashions displayed in the Bevis' parlor. She approved of the bridal gown of white dimity with a modestly low square-cut neckline that Lizzy Bartmess, Charlie's bride, wore. Wide bands of embroidery outlined the top and bust, forming a yoke. The puffed, short sleeves had double bands of embroidery ending in scalloped edges. A tight-fitting bodice held in place by a starched lining, ended in a point at center front several inches below the waistline. A vertical row of lavender velvet bows in front complimented the lavender forget-me-nots in the short veil of white tulle.

The bride's full skirt was sewn together in bias panels, flaring out at the bottom and ending in a plain hem. The gown was shorter on the right side (the side next to the groom). Two rows of embroidered bands inserted down the left-hand side of the white dimity skirt carried out the motif of the bodice trimming. The slim bride wore white kid slippers with spool-type heels. Her hosiery was white lisle. She carried a posy of pink rambler roses tied with a white satin ribbon bow. The bridesmaids, her sister Jane and friend, Milly Snyder, wore pink organdy.

After the ceremony, the merrymakers were so noisy indoors that they paid no attention to the ruckus the tethered horses made outside. Later, however, Alma and Opal said they remembered that they had heard the horses whinnying excessively, and some scuffling about. They ignored it at the time, assuming that the animals were a little spooked by the clamor going on indoors. Meanwhile Pa Bevis had invited the grown men to the pantry for a sample of his latest brew. He gave the boys the signal to begin the fun. There was a din of tin pans and wooden whistles, along with clanking cowbells, borrowed horns, and other noisemakers which the boys had put close by for the occasion.

The last wedding guests finally left early in the morning. Jim said his good-byes and was leaving when he heard Pa Bevis yell at his sons.

"Now, Alvin, you n' Levi are just carrying this shivaree charade too far!" He turned to Levi and said, "It's your chore to put my horse in his stall."

"But I did, Pa. I fed and watered Century first. Then I put the buggy in the shed."

Bevis took his lantern closer to a lone horse standing tethered to a post by the barn.

"Wal I'll be a consarned, daad-blasted dolt! Whose dadratted, son of a gun's nag is this? Run to the stall quick, Alvin, see if my sorrel is all right!"

Alvin returned hollering, "Century's gone Pa, but the buggy is still in the shed."

Jim had some doubts about it being a shivaree joke, although a switch of horses of such opposite value did look like the usual wedding prank, but he kept his suspicions to himself.

The next morning Century was still missing when Alvin went to hitch up the substitute nag to the rig so that his folks could drive to church. He almost ran out of breath running back to his father.

"Look here, Pa," he yelled. "Look what I found in the buggy," he said, holding out his hand, to show two big shiny gold slugs[2].

"Where at?" his father asked.

"Why, on the floor of the rig, close to the dashboard, next to the whip-socket," answered Alvin.

"Well of all the unspeakable gall I've ever seen in my years of horse tradin' this takes the swivel-tongued bridle bit! I might of sold Century for a hundred or a bit less, but I'm ashamed to be hitched to this poor puny plug that joker left me. Now I'll have to go to the trouble to get me another sprinter."

After the church meeting the next day, Hank reminded Jim that he and Ellie had left the shivaree early because their children were asleep in the back of the wagon on a pallet and Ellie kept running out every half-hour or so to see how they were. At no time did she hear or see anything unusual.

"Well, it musta bin soon after you all left that the animals were switched." Jim remarked. "Hank, you didn't happen to see what kind of nag Josh was riding did you?"

"Nope, don't even know where he tethered it."

The two friends decided on extreme caution considering that Josh's life was in the balance.

Jim walked over to the Bevis rig just as his father-in-law was getting ready to drive off. He patted the unwelcome horse on its face and jawbone, remarking, "He looks like an animal that would get you home safe all right. Have you found out yet who owns him?"

"Nope, an' I'm not about to look for his owner," Pa said. "Don't know if it's a slap at my skill as a horse trader but it saved me a lot of chinnin'. Besides, t'was the easiest horse-trade I ever made. Thinkin' it over, I'm satisfied. A hundred dollars in gold will buy me a good hunk of horseflesh. Anyways, the boys are kinda hankerin' after this rangy cayuse."

---

2 A gold slug is a slang term for a fifty dollar gold piece.

CHAPTER 18

JOSH RETURNS

Carl Hendricks, from the law firm of Bennet and Hendricks, remarked to his associate, "This year the spring has surely arrived like a roaring lion, but it's bound to go out like a lamb, calm and serene! Check these letters our client Josh Montgomery wants sent."

Bennet read it aloud,

March 22, 1901

Frank Coffee, Alva, Oklahoma Territory
Dear Mr. Coffee:

This letter is to advise you that the claim of eighty acres south of Alva, on which you have been growing crops, has now been patented by the original filer, Josh Montgomery.

He appreciates the work that you have done on it and desires to be generous. You, therefore, may keep all commissions on the crops due him, and the benefits accrued therefrom. That is on one condition: that you vacate forthwith said premises.

Attached hereto is a release, which you are advised to sign. It contains therein, a copy of the beneficiary letter that you gave to our client, Josh Montgomery.

Furthermore, we are constrained to advise you, that your forty acres near El Reno cannot be assigned to two persons. Viz. Gambell and Montgomery.

Please enclose, and return to this office the original beneficiary letter written on foolscap[1] paper that our client, Josh Montgomery, gave to you. From this day forward, March 22, 1901, it is rendered null and void. For your convenience we have enclosed a self-addressed, stamped envelope

---

1 A full foolscap paper sheet is 17 x 13 ½ inches. Foolscap was named after the fools caps and bells watermark commonly used from the fifteenth century onward.

Very truly yours,

Carl Hendricks, Attorney.

The second letter Josh Montgomery asked the lawyer to write was addressed to Levi P. Bevis as follows:

March 22, 1901,

Levi P. Bevis,
Alva, Oklahoma Territory.

Dear Mr. Bevis:
Our client, Josh Montgomery, wishes to advise you that on the night of your son's wedding he was in great haste, and not wishing to disturb the nuptial celebrations, he took your sorrel sprinter. He did, however, leave two fifty-dollar gold pieces on the floor of your buggy as earnest money.
He has returned to his patented homestead. The sorrel horse is now available for sale. If you are interested in taking possession of the animal he is giving you first chance to buy it back, if you so desire.
Very truly yours,

Carl Hendricks, Attorney,
Bennet and Hendricks, Attorneys at Law.

On the same day that Pa Bevis received his letter, there was another letter addressed to Mrs. Alma Bevis, which bore a Guthrie postmark. The return addressee was Mrs. Milt Coombs. Pa Bevis handed it to Alma, displaying considerable curiosity.

"Open it, Ma. Who is it from?"

Immediately she said, "It looks like Veny's handwriting. Guess she did marry that carpenter after all."

She looked up after reading two pages and remarked, "Veny says they are going to Kansas City, Missouri, where Milt has a few lots, and that he is going to build houses on all of them, at once. She says she is happy, but misses all the family. Says if you have forgiven her, they would like to come by here on their way to Kansas City, if we want them to. Oh Pa, It would make me so thankful if they could. Can I write her to come visit?"

Pa Bevis couldn't admit even to Ma how much he had missed his daughter and how sorry he was at his harsh words to her back in Kansas before the Race, so he cleared his throat a couple of times before replying to Ma's plea.

"Well, why not, Ma! Tell her to bring that carpenter husband along. Want him to show me how to build a small grain silo."

Lizzie was all aglow at the good news and the prospect of seeing her sister.

"Maybe we could have that overdue housewarming and make it a hoedown," she said enthusiastically to her mother. "Let's get the musicians together. If the weather is warm enough we could make benches and tables for eating outside."

She wondered if this marriage of Veny's was made in heaven, as she believed her own was. She reflected back to the first meeting with Jim when she looked down from picking apples at the Crouches in Pratt and saw him tether his horse at the hitching-rail. He walked over to the apple tree to tie up the cow that he was leading. Lizzie knew that only fate could have arranged it. In her confusion to see if her skirts were down, she dropped one of the apples she was picking right on his shoulders, spooking the cow. If Lizzie was surprised he was more so. She knew instantly she was looking at her future husband. But she feared in her own mind to confirm it. Afterwards, Jim told her that he had had the same feeling about her. It was love at first sight for both of them.

Now, in her role as mother, Lizzie was dominant, but in his field of husbandry, Jim made the decisions and she did not interfere. Their only difference was that Jim wanted to be more firm with the children. Lizzie had told him "I've seen enough of horsewhipping and hard use of the harness straps, and I don't want our young ones afraid of us like we were of my Pa."

"Unless discipline begins when the children are young, in their adolescent years they might get totally out of hand," he had answered.

When Pa Bevis brought Hendrick's letter over to Jim to read he asked, "What do you make out of this sentence? It says here about Josh: he has now returned to his patented homestead. Wonder what happened?"

"It does seem a puzzle." Jim commented, and read on. "Maybe he got the lawyer to get that fixed up too. I wonder how he got rid of the sharecropper Coffee? Guess I'll have to saddle up Barney this evening after supper and go over to see how it all came about. What do you aim to do about the sorrel? Going to take him back?"

"I've been thinkin' about that. Ain't got no replacement yet for Century. I'll have to see if he's as sound as he was when he left. If he stands up to a good inspection, I might offer Josh seventy-five dollars for him. A horse-trader like me ought to get something for the use of the animal. Besides, Century is some months older than he was. 'Course the boys won't want to let their buckskin cayuse go! If Josh will throw him in, I'd give him the hundred back."

When Jim tied Barney to the hitching post in Josh's yard there was another horse tethered there, a blue roan with a bald face and a white mane and tail. When he came up to the house he could see plainly that Josh was getting ready to plant corn. Two gunnysacks full of seed corn were leaning against the house under the stoop. At Jim's loud knock Josh opened the door.

"Why Jim, you old buffalo skinner! Glad to see ya! Come on in and meet Pete MacGuire, a feller I met on one of my travels. Pete's goin' to help me plant corn on shares. I'm furnishin' the land and team. He put up for the seed, and he's doin' half the work."

Jim held out his hand. "MacGuire, I'm glad to know you. Looks like a pretty good arrangement to me. Josh, I'm sure glad to see you're alive and well and back on the claim." Jim said it like he meant it.

"I got me a hired man, too," Jim continued with a grin. "Don't look like I'm goin' to get much help from three little girls and a son that's goin' to be too smart for hard labor. Dev is a Frenchman. It's short for Devereau. He worked on a canal down at the Isthmus of Panama that the French was building, but the French had to give up on account of malaria, yellow fever, and the money dried up. Dev tells some mighty entertaining tales of vile swamps, and the fact that many men are dying like flies down there. But I didn't come here to talk about that. Just want to let you, Josh, and you too, MacGuire, know that anything Hank and me can do, just call on us."

The three men left the house and walked to the hitching post. Jim untied Barney and turned to Josh and MacGuire.

"Got to be on my way, but Josh, sometime when you've got the time, I'd like to hear about your travels, especially this last trip." He pumped hands with each of them as he was leaving.

"Good meeting you, MacGuire. Josh, Pa Bevis will be seeing you soon about that sorrel you rode away on." Jim swung into the saddle and headed for home.

* * *

All spring Lizzie kept busy sewing on the treadle sewing machine she had gotten from Sears and Roebuck. She enjoyed making clothes for the children, now growing like magic before her eyes. She no longer sewed velvets for Robbie. He was too big for velvet suits.

Lizzie confided to Ellie, "I'm so thankful that I had Freddy and Rob dressed in their little Lord Fauntleroy suits with the ruffled blouses when that itinerant photographer came by, hoisting that picture-takin' apparatus. It's one thing I prize, that picture showing just how we all looked. 'Course I've got the picture of the two boys took before Freddy got sick. Pictures sure are a comfort."

Looking out from the front porch in the early morning, Lizzie thought she had never seen anything so beautiful as the blue morning glories twining around the pillars and up to the porch roof. Looking straight ahead, her eyes scanned a row of hollyhocks leaning against a fence that hid both the outhouse and a reserve woodpile. Nearby, a row of zinnias bloomed in a variety of colors. Despite her continuing inner grief at losing her 'come-see child', she now realized that gradually she had conditioned herself to his eventual departure ever since the day Granny Sullivan told her that an angel stood by to take him after he had seen enough of this world.

Nevertheless, there was much that Lizzie was grateful for, but most of all, she was grateful for her precious family and the farm. She no longer referred to their place as a claim, nor as a homestead, but as a farm. She recalled that back where she was born in Indiana anything larger than forty acres had been called a farm. She liked to think that their one hundred and sixty acres was a big farm. When she wrote to her maternal grandparents, the William Scranton Tower family of Indiana, the letter contained vivid descriptions of the flat topography, the creek and the many improvements to the land and the house of which she was extremely proud. Lizzie would also include anecdotes of Robbie and his three sisters.

CHAPTER 19

THE FARM

Threshing time at the Crouch farm arrived in full swing near the last week of May 1901. Either the Hartner, Bevis, or Crouch family would kill and dress a pig to be used to feed the harvesters. This year Lizzie and Jim furnished the pork. They decided to kill two red Duroc sows and a runty Poland China shoat. The latter, cut up and fried into cracklings would serve as a base for beans and greens to make a change from the usual sowbelly bacon.

On the chosen day, the Bevises and Hartners came to the Crouch homestead prepared to assist in the hog-killing drudgery. Each person present had a skill to contribute. Ellie's Pennsylvania Dutch parents had trained her in the art of spotless cleanliness, as well as in the economy of all aspects of family living, inside and outside the house. She knew how to utilize every scrap of pork for some particular use.

The back yard was converted into a food processing plant. Before the butchers began, they prepared huge copper vats of boiling water into which they would plunge the butchered pigs. Hank became the official pig sticker[1] for the occasion. It was easier to have a neighbor slaughter one of your own animals than to do it yourself, if there was the luxury of a choice. It was necessary that the animal bleed profusely. The farmers fed the blood back to the other pigs, and some of it was used in scrapple and blood sausage. In this case, the old adage was true, they did save everything but the squeal. They removed the hide, scalded the hair off, cleaned and tanned it for leather. The meat was butchered and selected for smoking, curing, or cooking as fresh pork.

The meat grinder was in constant use, and every man and boy present took turns in grinding the leftovers. The intestines were saved for sausage casings, following appropriate cleansing and steeping in brine. They ground the meat for sausages. Bratwurst, liverwurst and links were firm favorites within the group. Alma put

---

1 A pig sticker is a slang term for a butcher.

her prepared prairie sage and other seasonings in her batch of sausage. Everyone had pork steaks, roasts, chops, and spare ribs to take home. Ellie took the heads for making head cheese.

Pa Bevis liked to pickle the pigs' feet. Of course, before the lengthy pickling process could begin, the cloven hooves had to be cooked in boiling hot water to remove the outer layers of hoof and skin. They rendered lard as soon as they completed the butchering process and tossed pieces of fat into iron vats while keeping the fire underneath at a low temperature. The corkscrew tails could be barbecued over the coals. This day Ellie took the sow's tails and jowls home to make pepper-pot relish. Anything inedible for humans was saved for the dogs.

"Don't leave a scrap of evidence of what happened here today," Jim said, "or the varmints will descend on us in hoards!"

Dev, the hired man, had finished the building of a smokehouse where the hams and bacon would be hung. Lizzie and Alma were in charge of the smoking process, which would take several weeks of salting, smearing, and hanging in the smokehouse to cure before they could be kept all winter without refrigeration. Each family would receive a share of the operation.

The threshing crew was ordinarily mustered from the ranks of farmers, and farm hands from neighboring areas, and some workers from other states. Often comprised of one or more foreign members, seldom did the crew get to boast of two distinguished characters, which was the case this summer. Devereau, the Frenchman, who had worked at the Isthmus of Panama (where Ferdinand, Viscount de Lesseps, the architect and builder of the Suez Canal, had tried to cut a ditch through the narrow land mass between the Atlantic and Pacific Oceans), was a crew member extraordinaire. No less exciting in background was Jack O'Hara, who had fought in the Spanish-American War.

Although Dev had signed up as a harvester, he expected to return to the Crouches after the Cherokee Strip threshing contracts had been completed. At times he suffered from mild sieges of malaria, which had receded in the dry air of the Strip. His experiences in the tropics were tinged with frustration and as he recounted it in his heavy French accent, he made it sound real. Only someone who had actually been on the scene could describe the seething swamps, the tropical heat, unsanitary conditions, the rats, flies and vermin, the political absurdities and worst of all, the everlasting diseases.

O'Hara was a bit different. Though his tongue was glib enough, and the United States Army uniform that he occasionally wore fit his stalwart physique and sported the campaign medal on the left breast, Jim was never quite convinced that he was the O'Hara who had worn it in the battle of San Juan Hill. To hear O'Hara tell the story, he had ridden up to the top with Theodore Roosevelt himself. Jim was seldom taken in by heroic tales. He had an intuition that could separate the cream from the milk.

In his younger days, Jim had sat around too many campfires listening to lusty tales told as truth by wranglers who had no other evening entertainment except to top all of the adventurous tales told by the riders of the purple sage and solitary desert flats. It was true that in No Man's Land there were plenty of outlaws and various fugitives from the law. With prices on their heads, they valued their hides too much to let down their guard by giving away the true scenes of their escapades, their places of origin, or the direction in which they were heading.

Campfires cast a romantic glow, conducive to the secret revelations of a storyteller, be he a swaggering wrangler riding behind longhorns, or a harvester, after a hard day's labor of threshing wheat, or a cowboy pushing doggies[2].

On this particular night, most of the threshing crew, after a dip in the creek, hunkered down in a circle in front of the barn door. They built a smudge fire as a means of keeping the flying insects at bay. When the twilight faded, the eerie glow of the smudge-filled pot cast mysterious shadows against the double barn doors. The faraway screeching of an owl and the occasional yip-yip-yip of a pack of coyotes added to the background sounds. Jim passed papers around to the men who wanted to roll their own cigarettes. Others in the crew were smoking pipes, chewing tobacco, or using snuff. It was a nightly ritual to roll a fag[3] before turning in.

---

2 Doggies are unbranded orphan calves.

3 A fag is a slang term for a cigarette.

Pa Bevis ambled by and stayed briefly on his way to the sod house with a bucket of milk for the next morning's breakfast. Jim sat on his haunches with the rest of the crew, smoking his pipe.

"Well," said Bevis "seen in an old newspaper today that Queen Victoria of England died and that her profligate son, Edward the Seventh, is now on the throne. Guess he's already been rulin' since February, and here, none of us knowed it, nor gave a Continental about it. How many of ya wanta bet he won't ever be as good a monarch as the old queen was? Laugh about wimmin all ya want, but ya have to take yer hat off to that grand old lady."

Bevis snapped his galluses, spat out a 'cud of baccy' as he called it, and bid goodnight to the group. Jim would have preferred to stay and chin with the crew for a little longer, but there was too much to do. The crew had wanted him to tell them of his encounter with the Younger gang when they were part of Quantrill's Raiders then, but there would be another time before the crew would be moving on. Right now they certainly did need their rest. Jim got up, shaking his stiff ankles, and reminded everyone to get a good night's sleep and an early start in the morning. "Breakfast at 5:30, cook says you can have pork chops and hominy or codfish cakes 'n' eggs. Goodnight boys," he said as he left.

CHAPTER 20

HARVEST CREW

"Where did that old man Bevis learn such big words? Whadja s'pose he meant about the Prince, I mean the new British King Edward, bein' a pro-fli-gate? Does that mean he begat a bunch of illegitimate brats?" Jack O'Hara asked as soon as the boss left.

"I heerd tell of that word before," an older harvester called Bill said. "Guess Bevis got it from the Bible. Probably means the king is a big sport, likes boats, racehosses, wine, 'n wimmen. That old codger Bevis knows a heap. I also heerd when he was in that dirty old Confederate prison, along side him was an important officer passin' off as a common soldier, but he was some kinda spy for the Union, and that he saved Bevis's life, or maybe death, when gangrene set in his bullet-torn leg. This spy had some knowledge of herbs and medicine, but he had none of them to work with, not even rags to bind up the wound that was putrid an' foul-smellin'. The prison was servin' bread that was so rain-soaked and moldy that the prisoners couldn't stomach eating it. This feller tied some of the stale bread round the wound with a sleeve holder. It acted like a sponge, soakin' up the poison, 'til the leg got better."

The men watched him intently as he continued.

"Course Bevis was a strong husky man not yet twenty-one years old. His youth prob'ly saved his life. He was already a two-term soldier. Ott, his middle son, was tellin' me all about it just the other evenin' after I helped him to split some wood."

Two young hands, Comanche half-breeds, who were learning harvesting from the ground up, showed some interest in the tale.

Gray Cloud, nicknamed Cloudy asked "Whut happen to de officer? He git free from prison?"

The harvesters seemed surprised that the usually non-talkative Indians should show such awareness.

"Why don't you ask Ott, when you get a chance?" Bill said.

Running Deer, known as Deerskin, smiled and agreed that that would be a good idea.

With his engineering skills, Dev had shown Jim and Pa Bevis how to widen and deepen the creek so that their water supply would flow, even in times of drought.

While the threshing was going on at the Bevis homestead, the harvesting crew slept in the Crouch hayloft. No smoking of any kind was allowed inside the barn. Only a lighted lantern, hung from a hook near the entrance, gave light enough for the men to climb the ladder to the hayloft. The last one going to bed was charged with the chore of turning down the wick and blowing out the coal-oil light. Deerskin, Cloudy's younger brother, who could see almost as well in the dark as he could in daylight, assumed that duty. When he climbed the ladder his moccasins made no sound. Nor could he be heard as he wended his way down to the far side of the loft where the Comanche brothers slept apart from the rest of the crew under deerskins softened by years of use.

The hayloft was also Dev's hangout and sleeping quarters, which he was glad to share with the Comanche brothers for company's sake. Jim had given him a buffalo hide to sleep on, whereas the other hands carried their own bedrolls. Dev had read so much about the West that he was fascinated to be in close contact with these two Indians. He was interested in their language and culture. Dev had studied English along with Latin and Greek at the *école*[1] in Paris, but he was far from being a true linguist. He was beginning to learn colloquialisms, but at times he could sound comical when he mixed his formal expressions with local sayings. Nevertheless, he was eager to learn first-hand at least one Indian language, in addition to an American-English dialect.

At the end of the day Dev watched the Comanche brothers head to the creek for their usual dip in the cool water to wash off the dirt and sweat from the fields. He decided to join them, after making previous attempts at friendship with the brothers. He approached them and asked if he could join them, and so their mutual friendship began.

The next evening, after the three of them finished their ablutions in the creek, Dev asked to sit down with them under a

---

1 An école is a French school of higher learning for students heading into professional careers.

nearby cottonwood tree as he would like to get to know them better and learn about their Indian life and language. The brothers looked at each other then nodded in agreement. When they were sitting comfortably, Dev asked his first question.

"Since you are half white, why do you prefer to remain Comanche?" He asked. A long pause ensued.

"Squaw mother," Cloudy answered slowly. "Comanche, we be like her."

"Did she marry a white man?" Dev asked.

"She no marry. Father white scout. He no marry squaw mother. No see white father after Deerskin big papoose," Cloudy concluded in an indifferent manner.

Deerskin ventured more information. "We no live on reservation. You, no American, where you live?"

Dev took a well-worn map out of his pocket and unfolded it. The early twilight threw considerable light on the colored map. Dev pointed to North America, then to Oklahoma Territory, saying, "Here we are tonight. Right here."

He then moved his finger over to the Atlantic seaboard and down to the Gulf of Mexico. Finally, his finger traced east across the Atlantic Ocean to Cherbourg, in France.

"Here I was born and went to school. When I was twenty-two years old, after one year of study in Paris, I left France for Colombia, South America."

Tracing his finger across the Atlantic to Cartagena, he continued, "There, I signed papers to work in the engineering department of the Panama Canal Company, a French enterprise." He shook his head sadly, from side to side.

After Dev showed the Comanches the narrow strip of land between the Atlantic and Pacific oceans, they grasped the necessity of digging a ditch across the narrow land span. Cloudy spoke up.

"Your boat go through? Save time?"

"No. We failed. We only got started. It's very, very hot in the tropics. Swamps, vermin, disease. labor troubles, and then the Panamanians quit work. Colombia owned the land and Panama wanted independence. The money was all spent and the canal not dug. Men died like flies. I got malaria fever and the quinine medicine used to treat it ran out. I almost died. I got a North

American visa to get to New Orleans for medical treatment. It's the French Quarter where I lived. Almost like home."

The Comanches were awestruck. Dev was amazed by their comprehension. From what they had learned in a missionary school, and from the maps they had seen there, the meaning was just now coming to life. The concept of great distances and the mystery of far away places began to unfold and they fancied themselves traveling with the Frenchman in all his journeys. They felt sad about the failure of the project and the terrible fever he had experienced. They were glad, however, that he had come to the Oklahoma Territory now, and that they were working together in the wheat harvest. They began to feel a kinship they had never felt for any other white man.

"Squaw mother daughter of chief," Cloudy said. "Her grandfather heap beeg chief. Most terrible to white man. He hide from soldiers. White man no catch beeg Chief warrior. No got this chief. Very hostile Comanches."

"You don't seem hostile to me," Dev said. "Maybe white blood tames your spirits. What do you think?"

"Time no longer same," Cloudy wagged his head sideways. "We no go like other tribes in Indian Territory, we no fight in white man's war. We very hostile, fight each other like Indians on war path."

"You should keep Indian ways," Dev said. "Only take from white man what is good for both, for yourselves and them. I too, am learning from Americans, but don't want to lose my French culture. I always wanted to see the West. Ever since I read the story of Buffalo Bill and the expedition of Lewis and Clark, I wanted to see it. I planned to come here. I am glad to be here. In Europe we learn several foreign languages, we speak many tongues. I would like to learn one Indian dialect. Could you teach me a few words of Comanche?"

"How you learn sign language? We no write. Make picture talk. Make sounds. Name things. Dance. Spirit father listens. Sometimes tell us when do good things and bad things. Obey Spirit father, old chief, Man Above, up dere! But we teach you words, how to say?" Cloudy said, bowing.

"*Merci, merci.* That means thank you in French," said Dev.

"How you got here?" asked Deerskin.

"From New Orleans," Dev again pointed to the map. "Here, from town on the Gulf of Mexico, I took the train. I changed trains three times to get to Talequah, Indian Capital, where I signed up to work on a threshing crew. I worked the summer of 1900. I came back here and stayed with the boss all winter. He needed a ranch hand and I like clean fresh air out here and working outdoors. My malaria fever gets better in dry climate. I come back again after you go back to your land. Saving my money to go back to France one day."

"What you do in France?" asked Deerskin.

"Expect to write a book about the big Wild West, maybe, if I learn enough. I'm a civil engineer by profession."

"You come to our teepee?" invited Deerskin. "We show you Indian Spirit Dance."

"Merci, merci." Dev was overjoyed at the prospect of seeing intimate glimpses of Comanche life. "Maybe after we finish harvesting, and before I return here?"

"Sure. You go home with us. We show you way. Stay with us long time," Cloudy insisted.

CHAPTER 21

CLOSE CALLS

Two nights before the going away party when Jim was chinning with the hired hands, O'Hara asked to talk privately with him. Jack said he needed to send some money home and lacked ten dollars.

"Boss, since I expect to come back next year, if I left my dress uniform with ya could ya loan me that much? Then ya could take the ten bucks outa my first week's wages. A uniform like mine would cost three times that much, so it oughta be security enough, wouldn't ya say?" O'Hara explained as he made his request.

"Capital is pretty shy around here, especially after I pay out wages to all of you, but after the way you put it, I guess I can spare you ten dollars," said Jim reluctantly. "Suppose if you are sending it in the mail, you'd rather have a bill than a gold piece?"

Jack O'Hara handed over the uniform done up in a neatly tied package. Jim took out his elk-skin wallet, removed a federal gold-backed note of $10 and returned the wallet to his pocket.

"Boss," someone called, "ya ain't kept yer promise to tell us about them outlaws or bandits ya run into way back there, where wuz it? Quantrill, wasn't it, and the Youngers?"

Then someone else said, "What was the closest call you ever had?"

There were some things Jim Crouch was reluctant to talk about. One was politics, the other was saying evil against another fellow, and this was an occasion when both subjects had to be mentioned if he were to speak the truth as he judged it.

"Quantrill, the James brothers, and the Youngers really were all before my time. But some fateful fortune brought Quantrill and one of the Younger boys to my uncle's mountain home near Taylorsville, Kentucky, when I was a little tike no more than a year old. My mother was consumptive and most every summer we went there to get away from the stifling heat of Louisville. Kentucky, like Missouri, was a border state and felt the brunt of raids from the north and the south alike. The Civil War was supposed to be over by then, but hate on both sides was so het-up that folks just kept it up and lawlessness seemed to have neither rhyme nor reason. One night some people brought in Quantrill, sorely wounded. They patched him up, expecting him to survive, and they all left the next day. No one in the cabin actually knew that he was a general except he and the boys were fighting for the Confederates. He left behind a bag of personal items that he said someone would come for. My uncle treasured his obligation to keep them as he promised.

When I was five years old my mother died of the disease and my baby brother and I were shuttled back and forth with one relative after another until after I was seven. As long as the former slaves were alive, I stayed on in Martha's care on Pa's plantation. And old Martha taught me how to cook. Anyway, my brother Keene and I were back at my uncle's cabin in the mountains to spend what was left of the summer when I was twelve, going on thirteen, and Keene was about fifteen. One day, two strangers rode in, making some queries of us. When they found out that some of the Crouches were still there they tied up their mounts and came into the house. They stayed around there four or five days and remarked several times how much times had changed. Yet, I could feel a fire still burning inside them. Those men sounded like they were desperate, but I would swear they were not desperadoes. Keene and me held onto every word.

"Cole, the older brother, said at the time he knew our sympathies were with the wounded south and it wasn't difficult to cuss the damn Yankees. So the brothers felt right at home with us. 'Can't you see what a distinction it is that your home here sheltered one of the South's greatest fighters, Quantrill? It is such a shame he had to die, and on account of the Union guerillas, who found out who he was, drew a gun and shot him in the chest.' Cole said it like it only happened yesterday."

Jim licked his lips before he looked around him and took up the tale again.

"Then Cole looked Keene and me over and said, 'In another few years you boys will be big enough to ride with the best of us. We're not through with those Yankees yet, leavin' the South burnin' and the wimmin folks ravished. It'll never be restored in our lifetimes, so we've a mind to go give them some of their own medicine.'"

"At that minute," Jim continued, "I confess I wanted to help them. But after they left with the bundle of Quantrill's effects, including a little green tin box, my only thought was to get away from the sorrow of the South and go west. Three years after that we started west and you know about that. Except for when I lived with some relatives in Kansas for a few months and until I made the Run in '93, there was hardly a day I wasn't in the saddle."

"Did you ever see the Youngers or the James boys again?" asked Dev.

"No. The only time the James brothers figured in it, as far as I know, was when one of them helped to bring the wounded Quantrill into my uncle's place. By the time Keene and I rode as far west as Missouri, the Youngers were doing time in some prison up in Minnesota, or so we heard. At the time Keene said, 'Ain't it just like them! Breakin' into some Yankee bank to take their loot? Some people just cain't see things as they are, but as they want them to be.' That whole generation was so disrupted by their sense of injustice that they were unable to think straight," Jim continued.

"How do you explain that terrible raid on Lawrence, Kansas?" asked one of the harvesting crew. "Weren't the Youngers and Quantrill in on that?"

"You mean, when they burned the town and the women and children died?" Jim answered. "Why, they did that in revenge for what the Jayhawkers did when they raided Osceola, Missouri, and did the same thing to that town, and the women and children were the worst victims. That was the beginning of sorrows for the guerrillas with southern sympathies. Quantrill, they say, was a brilliant general, a crafty strategist and the kind of border raider that the Confederates admired. It didn't matter to them that he was part Indian as some said. He appeared as some kind of savior to the people of the border states who felt the hostile sting of those cursed Jayhawkers, whose deeds were as foul as any doggoned, lowdown scoundrel as ever drew a breath of life," Jim said, with more feeling than he usually showed.

He went on, "The Jayhawkers were forgiven by the states. Their crimes were canceled out, but not so for the guerrillas."

"You know, you seem to think Kansas was responsible for the Civil War," inquired Dev.

Jim thought for a moment, "As a matter of fact, I guess it did have a lot to do with the feelings of hostility in the whole nation, but each state had its own troubles, I suppose."

"We don't know exactly what you mean, boss. Some things you mention is over our heads, but if it's true what you say, it's a wonder there ain't more wars goin' on than there is," O'Hara observed.

"We all are influenced more than we want to admit by outside forces." Jim said. "I'm prejudiced, or was, I'll admit. But that's all over now. It's too late to turn back and change anything now. We are all Americans. The West is a new order, and thank God that it is."

Jim thought that he had learned more compassion and forgiveness from Martha than he realized until that moment.

"The French thought the South had justice on their side and were ready to come to her aid had the conflict been prolonged." Dev remarked knowingly.

Ott, who was listening, had never heard before that there was more than one side of the Civil War question to be discussed. He wanted to interject a few words on his father's behalf, but was too shy to know how to put it except to say, "Well, we preserved the Union."

Bill, a harvester, who up to that time had only listened, managed to give some views of his own, "As someone that's lived longer and had more experience, I'd say, looking into the future a hundred years or more hence, the nation is apt to still be divided from consequences of this unholy war. First, the cream of the crop on both sides was killed off. When the white population gets thinner and the black population increases, who will take over the reins of the nation? Lincoln said he was against blacks ever having the vote, or sitting on a jury, but the majority can force public opinion. Fellas, our grandchildren are in for bad times. Almost half of the nation believes that had Stephen Douglas been elected President, instead of Lincoln, that there would not have been this mess. Douglas believed that the issue of slavery could have been settled without war. It's no crime to admit that, if this is a free country, is it?"

Jim decided it was time to change the subject. Everyone had had his say, anyway.

"Fellers, you asked about my closest call. I guess you all noticed how I treat Barney, my old cutting hoss, more like one of the family. Well, indirectly he saved my life once. That was when he was just a foal, not even weaned yet. His roan coat showed the Appaloosa wild strain, and though the mare had some Morgan and thoroughbred strain she could cut in and out of the herd as good as any gelding. I used her once on a trail when my regular mount was laid up with a stone bruise. Barney tagged along of course, and I watched him trotting and galloping around like a thoroughbred. His white mane was just growing out and showed off the white speckles on his rump. When he kicked up those white stockings of his he showed real class. I said to myself, if I don't watch out someone is going to try to buy him from me, but I'd be a fool to part with him for any price. Right there I made up my mind to keep him and break him gradually without breaking his spirit. I even considered keeping him a stallion, as he was pretty enough. 'Course working horses, as you know, have got to be gelded. Can't trust stallions on long trails."

Jim stood up to stretch his legs, sat down again and continued. "The boss sent me over to a border township to get some strays. There was a line shack where I could bunk in for the night before turning back to the main ranch, which would take four or five days, all told. I don't know how many thousand acres the outfit had but a feller could ride for days without seeing another soul. I'd been out only a day and a half I guess, when up rode a stranger. At first I thought it was one of the cowhands, until he asked me how to get out of there.

"Before I answered him I saw that he was riding a fine mount, a young Morgan, if I know horseflesh.

"Well, stranger," I told him, "you better turn around and go back the way you came." He just sat there in the saddle for a moment with his hand on his holsters.

"Then, without flinching a muscle he said, 'That's a pretty fine mare you're ridin'. He went on, 'Like the looks of that colt too. I'll swap my full blood Morgan for'm.'"

"Nope," I replied. "I need my steed for just what she's trained to do."

"'Why, you're not a very good businessman,' the stranger said. 'You know you should be able to sell this mount I'm on for twice what yours is worth. Tell you what I'll do, since it's the colt I fancy I'll give you five dollars to boot. We'll change horses, and I'll give you the five dollars in gold,' and he held out the shining gold coin in the palm of his hand."

"Nope, I said." Jim tended his pipe and looked around at his appreciative audience and took up the tale once more.

"I fancy this colt myself. In a year, I said boastfully, I'll have this colt harness broke, and another couple of years after that, he'll be cutting out mavericks as good as this here mare, I answered, patting her shoulders. Then I gave her the spur and off I rode. Looking back afterwards, I began thinking that the stranger didn't fit his fine horse. He slouched in his saddle and wore a straggly mustache and beard. He musta been a younger man than he looked at first glance. I felt kinda funny that only a few minutes before he appeared I had decided to keep Barney, like it was some kind of warning. Not over a range away I saw dust rising from two riders, and thinking to myself, this country is getting to be more than a cow-path these days, I rode on.

"Well, it wasn't more than three days later when I came back the same way and not far from where I met the stranger, that I saw something from a distance that looked like a scarecrow, and vultures circling overhead. Round about they wheeled overhead, just scouting that thing clinging to the scrub tree below. A few minutes later when I came closer I saw the dreadful sight of a man hanging from a rope and his feet dangling not a foot from the ground. It was a horrible sight, with flies a-swarming all over his eyes, nose, and mouth. The stench was so bad I hated to get any closer. His features were so swollen I didn't recognize him at first. Then it suddenly dawned on me that he was no other than the scroungy looking stranger that wanted to swap horses with me. Yep, there was no doubt about it. I picked up his tattered hat and threw it up on his head and then he looked more natural. That act was a protection from the noonday sun for what would remain of the decomposing corpse. Not that it mattered. Chances were that he would hang there, with the buzzards, flies and ants picking his rotten flesh before any lawman would come to investigate. I surely intended to report all I knew about it.

"When I got back, the ranch foreman gave me time off to make my report in town. The sheriff of that district said that some strangers were holed in one of the line shacks down in the Cheyenne Arapaho Nation all winter, but they had come out in the spring and later one of them was missing. He said there had been some horse thieves operating in the vicinity. Rumor had it that some of the Dalton Gang hid out over there when things got too hot in the Indian Territory. I asked the sheriff if he had any pictures of wanted men to show me. But there was none I recognized when I looked."

"He told me, 'Just you let us know who the renegade was if you ever find out.'" Jim paused momentarily to knock the ashes from his pipe. Then he looked at the men watching him attentively.

"Oh, I forgot to mention, that pinned on his duck jacket with a fence staple was a small sign that read HOSS-THEEF."

"That sure was a close call," cried O'Hara. "If you'da traded mounts, who d'ya s'pose would a bin hangin' there instead?"

"There's no doubt about it," Jim said. "Rustling and horse thieving are about the worst crimes a fellow can commit. Horse owners are the hottest-headed of the lot. Vengeance cuts deep. They act first and think later. I'm positive now I saw from a distance those hangmen. Maybe if their dust hadn't abeen kicking up, the stranger might have tried to force me off my mare and then he would have gotten away with it. Then you know whose head woulda been in that noose, and you wouldn't be hearing this tale. God, what a horrible way to die!"

The harvest crew called "Good night, boss," as Jim strode away.

CHAPTER 22

HOEDOWN

Coinciding with the arrival of sister Veny and her new husband, Lizzie and Jim planned not only a fitting welcome for them, but a hoedown party for the departing harvest crew and a house-warming all combined in an affair of major proportions. They invited all their neighbors, especially those with marriageable daughters so they could meet eligible bachelors, knowing that most matchmaking was made at such social gatherings. Charlie and his bride Lizzy invited her two sisters. Two of the local harvesters had sisters whom they had mentioned in extravagant terms to other crews. This would be a splendid occasion to bring them together, expecting Cupid to do the rest.

The guests who had musical talent brought their instruments and were invited to play anything from an Irish Jig on the jew's harp to the Virginia Reel on the fiddle. This frolic would fling the buck and wing[1] crowd out of the hayloft and bring them reveling into the parlor fandango.

Hank and his talking banjo arrived first. He took over as musical director for the evening. Neighbors Benecke, with his old-world accordion, and Barry Werner, carrying his guitar, arrived together. Two other fiddlers, asked to act as substitutes while the others danced arrived early to get Hank's instructions. Jim, if needed, could fiddle as relief musician, especially for the singing.

Veny and Milt were pleased to be the honored guests at the Crouches' first dance given in their impressive new home. Lizzie had put the children to work making colored tissue paper chains to hang from the ceiling center to the outer walls. Opal and Robbie strung popcorn strands across the porch pillars. There was a festive air about the entire setting. The Bevis boys had set up stakes dipped in coal oil for lighted torches.

A sweet pungent fragrance permeated every room in the house bedecked with roses and lilacs from the garden. Tantalizing aromas

---

1 The buck and wing is a fast tap dance.

of fried chicken, baked ham and venison, compliments of the hunting skills of the Bevis boys, along with the many savory dishes contributed by the guests, greeted visitors already hungry from the long ride in the open air.

Opal looked beautiful and more grown-up in her white, three-quarter length organdy dress. Stationed near the front door she served apple cider, buttermilk, or a mild punch made from syrup extracted from sand plums. She was told to remain at her post until everyone was seated. However, her prankish brother Ott asked her to go into the kitchen to bring something out for her mother. During her brief absence, he spiked the plum punch with his father's home-brewed plum jack and served it to the vivacious younger crowd, already bursting with energy.

Following the arrival of the musicians, country cousins and other guests poured in. The only late-comer was Sven Ulric, the coronet player who had to retrieve his brass horn from Alva's only loan shark. He rode up on a brass-bedecked chestnut charger yodeling his arrival. Ott greeted him with a mug of spiked punch. Ott figured that his pa was not about to take a blacksnake[2] to him now, him so grown-up and all.

Lizzie clapped her hands for attention and invited, "Find seats everyone."

Jim, smiling at the other end of the big table said, "Folks, it sure is good to see you. We are grateful the Lord has provided us with such fine friends and neighbors. Now, please help yourselves to the grub."

No one was bashful. The chitchat stopped. Everyone began eating at once. It was not long before second helpings of food were brought in from the kitchen and these summarily disappeared.

"Save your forks, everyone," Lizzie reminded them. "There will be your choice of shoofly pie, ginger cake, or cottage cake with cherry sauce and a few other sweet dishes. For those with bear appetites, there is plenty for second helpings."

Later the chairs and tables were pushed back, the Axminster rugs rolled up, and the long space between the dining room and the

---

2 A blacksnake is a flexible leather whip.

parlor was opened up for dancing, amid noise and lively confusion. Jim, clapping his hands, got the crowd's attention. The wave of conversation died down after a few seconds, so that he could be heard.

"Folks, Lizzie and I wanted to celebrate the turn of the century here with a house warming, but as you know, things happen that you don't count on. Now, we have finally gotten you all together to welcome back Lizzie's sister Veny and her spouse, Milt."

When the applause ceased he continued, "But this shindig is for a double reason. The harvest hands are leaving at dawn in the morning. They worked hard and long hours to reap, thresh, and bind our wheat crop, and some even drove the wagons to the granary in town. We want them to know how much we think of them, and how much we want them to come back next harvest."

He remained standing, and added, "Folks, we've got some unusual talent here tonight. It's too soon after dinner to sing and dance, so the Comanche brothers, who worked right along with the other hands in this best of harvests, have agreed to treat us to a hunting chant on their tribal buffalo horns. Their grandfather, old Chief Black Wing of untamed fame, might not like what they are doing here tonight, but I know we're sure going to. Friends, here are the boys: Cloudy and Deerskin."

The brothers had just returned from the barn, where they had dressed in their tribal regalia. An "Oo-ah!" sounded through the crowd. Rarely before in the Cherokee Strip, had white settlers had social communication with Indians, but Jim gave them no time to think or act.

After Cloudy whispered something in his ear, Jim announced, "Why don't we go outside to watch them blow the buffalo horns? The Comanche brothers think they would be too loud indoors." Everyone followed Jim and gathered outside on the porch.

A long clear strong sound broke the air barrier. There followed a series of strange staccato notes. A crescendo of drawn-out wails that gradually diminished in volume sent shivers rippling along the spines of the audience. The enthralled crowd gave the two musicians an enthusiastic applause when they ended their performance. Dev smiled triumphantly.

The guests reentered the house ready to dance. The musicians tuned up. Ott and Molly were the first pair to step out on the floor expecting a waltz, popular at that time. Despite his injured hand, Jim grabbed his fiddle and Hank his banjo and began to play before Benecke could strap his accordion straps over his shoulders. They had danced through the first stanza of Little Brown Jug, when some bold cowpoke jumped to the center of the floor and started to jig. Encouraged by this, another youth leapt out and began doing the buck and wing, oblivious to the beat of the music. The dance artist, as he fancied himself to be, needed only to stomp, kick and buck until soon he was out of breath, and then he retreated, a little bashful at his own boldness.

The long awaited waltz began and suddenly the floor was crowded with dancers. The three-four beat relaxed and quieted the dancers, and they clapped for an encore. Some of the musicians had come from the old country, and they were familiar with Johann Strauss and his lilting music.

Benecke rose to stretch his legs after they had played the Blue Danube and Tales from the Vienna Woods. "Tonight," he said, "we have brought you some of the gaiety and beauty of Vienna right into the heart of the Cherokee Strip. I wish Vienna could see us here but I wish, someday, that all of you will be able to see the gaiety and the magic of Vienna." His cheeks looked very pink and he blew his nose rather loudly into a big red kerchief as he moved on into the crowd.

A wallflower from the back of the room stood up and called for the Virginia Reel. Another rose and hollered, "We want to square dance and here is Quinlen, the best caller on the Strip." They danced the reel and Quinlen called several sets of square dancing. The dancers seemed tireless. Alma thought they would never go home, so she told Lizzie that she was ready to turn in, but she would return to help her with the clean up in the morning.

Pa Bevis invited several of the older menfolk to join him on the side-porch of Jim's house where they could enjoy their tobacco, partake of Pa Beavis's homemade sand plum brandy, or as he called it, his "fermented schnapps", and it was their custom to also discuss the local and national events when they got together.

"This is pretty fair stuff," said old man Snyder.

"Stouter than that other batch," remarked Ben Sullivan.

Sullivan was an old friend of Jim's from Ponca City and had been in the Race as well.

"What's happenin' in the world, Ben? You take a weekly newspaper from Wichita, don't ya?" Pa Bevis queried.

"The papers are full o' that yaller fever cure made by an army doctor, feller by the name o' Walter Reed," Ben answered. "That's what defeated the French in diggin' the canal down there in Panama. The British want to go in with us to dig a canal, but Congress won't hear of it. What's Britain got stickin' her nose in it, they say? McKinley wants the government to buy out the French railroads down there that are rusting away, and then we can dig the canal ourselves. Course, we gotta pay Colombia for the land and straighten out the mess between her and her province, Panama. One thing is sure, they'll have to import more diggers 'cause the Panamanians won't go back to work. They know that a man cain't live very long in them swamps."

"How about that gold rush in Alaska a couple of years ago? Anything much come of it?" one of the men asked.

"Papers let that die down," Pa Bevis answered. "Too many men returning frostbitten and disappointed, I guess. When the Democrats nominated Bryan and Adlai Stevenson on the free silver issue, gold took the limelight again. McKinley said that the rest of the world wouldn't be in support of silver at a fixed price, so the Republicans got a bill passed. The Gold Standard Act, I think they call it."

"How in the world will that affect us, way out here in the sticks?" another man wanted to know.

"The Act will make our United States coinage the strongest and safest in the world," Pa Bevis responded. "No matter what happens, a man can take his silver or paper dollars into the bank and demand gold in exchange, if he wants it. That oughta make fer prosperity after that '97 panic. We have a feller named Theodore 'Teddy' Roosevelt for Vice President now. He's the hero of the Spanish American war. Teddy the Rough Rider, he's called. We have some old papers here, if ya'd like to glance over 'em. Dated April and May 1901."

The men leafed through the papers, picking out an occasional item here and there for discussion or information. An item about the Boxer Rebellion in China absorbed their attention. Paraphrased, it indicated that the United States favored an open door policy, preventing China from being divided up among European powers, as so many unexplored lands had been. The Islands of Hawaii had been annexed to the United States almost a year earlier with a commentary on the advantages of a Pacific Ocean base. There was mention of a new count of victims of the 1900 Galveston hurricane and flood. Last but not least, a sports item described the plans for the founding of an American Baseball League.

Meanwhile, back at the main house, the young crowd was still tripping the light fantastic. The musicians had their turn also, dancing one quadrille after another. Ott became a victim of his own prank. He proposed to Molly Snyder, known throughout the south township as a girl of ready wit and as something of a spitfire. She accepted him on the spot, without a hint of maidenly reticence. The young bucks glided and the does fluttered in a frolic few of them would forget. Their elders finally called for an end to the merriment. Some people had morning chores, and that meant no sleep at all. The coal oil lanterns were burning low, and their sooty shades dimmed the light. The torches had burnt out and it was difficult to see, but everyone left without mishap.

Lizzie smiled happily as she hugged Veny when Milt brought her to say goodnight before they retired to the Bevis home. During the evening Veny had confided to Lizzie her satisfaction in being welcomed with her husband as part of the family once more. The exchange rewarded Lizzie and amply repaid all of her efforts. She reflected that they had celebrated the new century along with their lovely new home and Veny and Milt's presence enhanced the experience for everyone. Yes indeed, the party was worthwhile, Lizzie told herself with pride.

Dev stayed to help Opal who had put on Lizzie's apron to protect her white dress, which did not diminish her beauty in his eyes. He moved furniture while she swept the floor of fallen party debris.

"Opal," he said softly, "you don't know it in your innocence, but you are a perfect American beauty. I couldn't keep my eyes off you. If I were a few years younger, and had a castle somewhere, I'd carry you away to it and make you its mistress. As it is in reality, I'm just a harvest hand leaving in the morning with the crew. But I'll tell you this: I'll come back for you some day, if you've a mind to wait. Will you do me the honor of writing to me? Will you answer my letters when I write?"

"Oh, yes indeed!" Opal replied, blushing furiously. "I'm honored that you paid attention to me. You're from across the sea and know so much. Pa speaks of sellin' and goin' to town where my brother Alvin and me can go to the Normal School. Sometimes I help the teacher with the small children when they are learnin' from the McGuffy's Reader. My teacher gives me books to read. She says I ought to go to a school of higher learnin'! My sister Veny says I can live with her and go to school in Kansas City. But Pa says she wouldn't be strict enough."

"What are you trying to tell me, Opal?" Dev said earnestly. "That you're not desirable as you are? Don't go to Kansas City. Some rich Lochinvar would be sure to snatch you right out of my arms. If these were feudal times you wouldn't even know how to read and write, and you would still be a great lady."

"Don't put such grand notions in my head, Dev. You know it cain't be that way. I wouldn't want you to be ashamed of my ignorance. I like to learn and I intend to keep up my readin'. I even believe I might learn some French. Are you sure you will return next harvest, Dev? I do like you a lot."

"It is my expectation to return, Opal. I suppose I should go home to France and begin my career of journalism or engineering, but two things oppose it; this undulant malaria and you, *ma cherie*."

He stepped a little closer, but Opal moved back when she heard footsteps enter the kitchen from outside and she began to sweep the floor industriously to cover her emotions.

Pa Bevis came into the dining room and, glancing quickly at his daughter and the Frenchman, he turned to Devereau.

"Oh, here you are, Dev. Want you to see this old newspaper. There's a lot in here about a yellow fever cure. Knew you'd want to learn about it. Seein' as how you was down at the Isthmus when the plague broke. There's a whole lot of other news, but most of it so far away that it don't matter much to folks around here. Ben Sullivan left his paper with me and I'm finished. Take it along."

"Pa, Dev was goin' to walk me to the sod house."

"Well, let him come along with us," he answered. "I think he ought to be getting some sleep too, knowin' he has to get up before dawn. What am I talkin' about? Why it'll be dawn in about another hour's time, I guess."

"Well, here we are already," Pa Bevis remarked fifteen minutes later as they walked up to the Bevis sod house. "Goodnight, Dev. See ya' before you leave."

With that brusque farewell, Pa Bevis escorted Opal through the doorway.

"Good night, Dev!" she called back over her shoulder.

"Good night, Opal. Will I see you later this morning?"

"I hope so," she answered.

Dev returned to Jim's barn with a sad little smile on his face thinking how much alike papas were all over the big broad world.

When Opal arrived to help Lizzie later that morning she found most of the clean-up work already done. She had slept four hours without awakening. She was both chagrined and terribly disappointed that she missed saying good-bye to the harvesters when they departed.

"Oh, Opal," her Pa called from the dining room. "Come out from the kitchen. I've got something that someone left for you."

"Who was it? Devereau?"

"Of course it was Dev. Who else around here reads books?"

He handed them to Opal with the observation, "Dev said this one is written by a woman. The other one is by Charles Dickens. Want to read it myself too, if ya don't mind. Dev said he'll be back for 'em in the fall, and that ya might as well read 'em. That Jane Eyre book is prob'ly a lot of nonsense."

Opal hugged the books to her breast. At least she had something personal that belonged to Dev. While she read them she could dream of discussing the contents with him on his return. It was so much better than no contact at all.

CHAPTER 23

OPAL

Several days after the harvesters left, Opal received a picture postcard of the Northwestern State Normal School in Alva from Devereau. Two months later she received his first letter. He mentioned his eagerness to return and that he would be eternally grateful to her if she would convey his sincere good wishes to her parents and to all of the family, in whose homes he had been made to feel so cordially welcome. In contrast to the rather formal letter, he poured out his pent-up feelings in a postscript. He had gone to the Comanche brothers' teepee and had already spent over two weeks with them.

Opal,

If white people would only open their eyes and ears they would learn many helpful things from the red man. I have been taken into their confidence, and they are teaching me unheard-of secrets. It will be hard for anyone to understand their closeness to nature. It is as though they penetrate another dimension that is closed off to us. Maybe we have it, but have failed to use it.

I am certain that you will hear more from Deerskin and Cloudy. These Comanches couldn't be tamed by warfare! But by your folks' kindness they are becoming what you call civilized. They never wanted to know very much about white people before. Now they want to plant wheat, kaffir corn, broom corn and maize to make dough (ha! ha!) wampum. In other words, they want to put away the drums of war and become commercial farmers in the best tradition of the white man.

The letter closed with words of affection and eagerness to see her again soon. Opal found herself daydreaming on two levels at once. She was thinking of Dev, but she found her mind wondering about his closing words.

Early one splendid morning in mid-September 1901, Opal supervised the three older Crouch children in the meadows where the stock grazed. Each carried an empty gunny sack in which to put the dry cow chips they would be gathering. Nature had been more than generous in supplying self-sufficiency in the northwestern portion of the Strip where no trees grew. From the first days of homesteading, dried buffalo chips afforded the only fuel other than brush to burn for cooking and heating. Later on, coal, and occasionally wood were available fuel.

While the children went about their task, Opal took three letters and the postcard from her pocket. She touched them with fondness and a gentle look came into her eyes as she thought about Dev. Although she had read them at least twice she wanted to be alone when she read them this last time. She would evaluate every word and try to come to a decision about her future behavior and direction. She told herself that she could think better if only these pesky flies wouldn't torment her. She hugged little Mabel who came over for a moment's rest. Alone once again, Opal opened the second letter and read:

Dear Friend:

You cannot imagine what a different world it is from anything I've seen or ever known before, to be living with the Comanche brothers. I believe I have gotten under their skin as they have under mine. They have initiated me into their tribal rites and I am their blood brother. I have smoked their pipe and have partaken of the sacred Paiute cactus buds[1] that the shaman brings from a location far away from the tribe.

I think it is poisonous, for I was deathly ill at first. A malaria attack followed, but after two days, I felt completely free.

The shaman presided over the beginning of the rites but he was the first to fall into a deep trance. Some of the long deceased chiefs talked through his lips to those present, and frequently offered them advice for behavior in the new century. When Cloudy interpreted it to me, I concluded some of the information was for my benefit. I'm sure Deerskin and his older brother know all about

---

1 The cactus buds may have been related to peyote which has a long history of ritual religious and medicinal use by indigenous Americans. It flowers from March through May and sometimes as late as September.

nature spirits and the secret of the winds, rains and hoarfrost, while I do not.

Nothing happened for quite a while after I ate the tiniest bud. Then, for several hours I thought I would die, before I felt any effects from the bitter stuff. Finally my stomach returned to normalcy, and at that time I must have swooned. Perhaps I, too, became entranced for I'll swear that good-sized gnomes arose from the ground with the ability to run, hop, and jump.

Then I looked skyward and what did I see but lovely sylphs floating about in the air, dancing and singing like the wind through the trees. But the strangest thing of all happened. An old Comanche chief, Black Wing, entered our dimension of life. Black Wing has been dead a whole decade. He whooped and hollered with the vitality of a young buck. There was much more of this illusion, but the rest I will tell you personally when we meet.

Deerskin presented me with a gorgeous pinto we call Piebald, because he has a bald face except for a brown star on his forehead. I'm going to ride him over to your place when I return later this year. Deerskin caught this wild stallion himself and then broke him to ride. I enjoy riding bareback. It takes a little skill, but once you get used to it, you certainly feel at one with the animal. He says there are lots of wild horses in the Wichita Mountains, only it takes a good deal of patience to catch one. Just think! I'm tracking with the real Plains men where the buffalo roamed and where Jim rode as a wrangler in his youth. I can just see him driving those huge Longhorn herds from Texas to Dodge City in the old days. For a Frenchman like me to get this far West is quite an accomplishment. I'd like to tell my countrymen about it, but I'm afraid that my father will want me to get back to engineering. I've seen so much that I want to tell it on paper first hand.

I'll have something to say to you, Opal, my American Beauty. I'm counting on your advice.

Your admirer,
Dev

Opal then opened the last letter with a sigh, as if it were painful to read.

Dear, dear Opal,

I've had very bad news from home. My father is gravely ill and I must depart this country at once. If things were different I wouldn't leave without you. I will write to you just as soon as I can. I would like to ask you to wait for my return, or UNTIL I could send for you, but that may be at least a year. I would like to speak out, but it would not be fair to you, to ask you what I had in mind. Keep the books that I gave to your father, and someday I hope to send you a couple more that I have on my bookshelves at home.

May I trouble you to tell your brother-in-law, Jim Crouch, about the sad news about father and say how sorry I am not to return this winter to help him? I am sure there are others who can fill my job as well.

Now, cherie, until I can write from across the sea, I am,
Yours devotedly,
Dev.

The inner struggle engrossing Opal that serene morning was far more serious than the exterior discomforts caused by flying insects. It was the first important decision with affairs of the heart that she had to cope with. It seemed impossible to come to any definite conclusion. The question in her mind was her ability to wait a span of months, or years, if need be, for another meeting with Dev. She asked herself in earnest if he would remain faithful considering that he had not really declared himself. She wondered if it were actually true that absence makes the heart grow fonder, or if the opposite, that absence caused the heart to wander, was nearer the truth. Perhaps absence only made the heart grow fonder for people who had known each other after a long association, and their friendship, precious though it was, had been of such pitifully short duration. On the obverse of the coin, would she, herself, be equal to the task of fending off the passionate onslaughts of young men seeking her favors? Would she be able to parry their advances? Opal was perceptive, if inexperienced.

Opal remembered with deep satisfaction that she had been eagerly sought after by the young bucks at the hoedown. Of course, she reminded herself, a dance is not a reliable place to judge. On that night her eyes had beheld no one but Dev. Given a chance, she was certain that feeling the force of attention from Sven, or even Fritz, she could be prompted to return their affection.

She recalled with pleasure how she responded when Sven had said "Why, Opal, you look like a dream in that fluffy white." And when he asked, "We'll dance again at the box supper?" she knew that she had that to look forward to.

"No doubt about it, Opal, in my eyes, you are the queen of the ball," Fritz had said.

While sitting there on the dry grass, her legs folded under her, Opal determined to wait for two months before coming to a decision. That would give her time to receive a letter from Dev and to evaluate his attitude toward her from a distance. Meanwhile, she would go to the box supper but she promised herself that she would not encourage anyone while her heart still belonged to Dev. She called the children and they came dragging their filled gunnysacks behind them.

CHAPTER 24

LITTLE GLADYS

On the way to the barn Gladys found a little cottontail caught in a thicket on the lower strand of a barbed wire fence. His fur was torn on the shoulder where she saw its bare skin. She freed it from the wire and took it home to her father to heal. He saw at once that it was emaciated and if it did live it would be easy prey to other beasts, so he put it out of its misery. It was both a sad and unfortunate circumstance that he did not have time to explain this to the child. She grieved inordinately.

Who knows, or even cares, in this land of excess rabbits whether this act of killing a small animal would affect the wild kingdom? But there is no doubt that it did affect the attitude of the child toward her father. She no longer thought of him as a peerless man who could do no wrong. The rapport she had felt toward the bunny still lingered. It was akin to the way she felt when she sat on the back of old Barney, a oneness of identity. The little one climbed up in the Studebaker wagon and she sobbed herself to sleep. Gladys knew her babyhood was behind her.

In late September the neighborhood gathered for a box supper. These events were held in the little red schoolhouse about once a month. The terrible news of President McKinley's assassination was just reaching the area via the telegraph and the newspapers. There were only a handful there that had been alive at the time of Lincoln's assassination, but they repeated their recollection of that tragic event and compared it with what they had heard of the McKinley affair, concluding both murders were committed by raving madmen. One theory that stayed in Bevis' mind was that Lincoln, ever set on retaining the coinage of money in the control of Congress, as the Constitution had provided, bucked the international financiers. Some contended that they were the enemies who wanted Lincoln out of the way. In the case of McKinley, it was admitted that his assassin belonged to a foreign group labeled by Americans as IWWs, the I Won't Work class.

The Cherokee Strippers, as they called themselves sometimes, grieved for McKinley, for his administration favored the opening of land to white people. From what they had heard they were willing to give the new president Theodore Roosevelt every opportunity to prove himself.

"It's too bad that Jack O'Hara isn't here to strut and shout about the trek he made up San Juan Hill with Teddy himself!" Jim said. "That ought to make him come running to pick up his dress uniform that I'm holding for the ten dollars he borrowed from me."

Opal was not the only one testing out the box social. The spinster[1] school teacher, Bertha Bradford, wrapped up her box with a piece of wallpaper that had fancy flowers on a pink background design, and a pink satin bow to match. It sure was hard to tell from appearances just how good the food was inside the box. All sorts of bribery was going on to ascertain just whose box was worth the bidding. Ott had slipped into the kitchen to see how Opal's box looked. She had hinted to him that either Fritz or Sven would be acceptable as a supper partner, but when her box, tied with a red ribbon came up for auction, both of the young men were out-bid by a stranger. He had come from Alva with some friends who worked with him at a gypsum mine. He was a miner and was well paid for his skill. He tried to sweep Opal off her feet but she kept to her decision not to encourage anyone for the time being.

If the days on the prairie were often dry, dusty and monotonous, the nights were just the opposite. The air had a clarity and purity combined with unobstructed visibility. The starry skies shone with a splendor seldom seen anywhere else. Ever since Gladys was four years old, night after night she made a practice of going outdoors alone. Sometimes when she heard the yip, yip, yip of the coyote and the hoot of the owl sending chills down her spine, she would rush back into the house to bed. But when the nights were serene, she gazed fascinated at the starry heavens, wondering in her childlike way, how large the stars really were and whether there were people living on them. She wanted an answer more than anything. Looking at the heavens she saw a world apart from her own world. She would ask for answers from her

---

1 In that time and cultural setting, a woman was considered of marriageable age at 16. An unmarried woman over twenty was termed an old maid or a spinster.

grandfather. After all, she'd been told he knew the Bible backwards and forwards.

"Grandpa," Gladys began, "What part of the heavens do you suppose Freddy went to in his heavenly home?"

He looked at her strangely and said "Well, mankind down here knows very little about life on other planets. Even the astronomers cain't figger or fathom much 'cause, I s'pose, our minds are mortal human. The Bible says God is spirit, an' so are we, I guess, but the flesh seems to have crowded out our spiritual understandin'. The most we kin hope for is to have faith that some day, God willin', all things will be revealed to us, here or hereafter.

"I remember in Job, when all the wise men failed to explain things to him that the Lord answered Job out of the whirlwind. He revealed many secrets and asked, 'Canst thou bind the sweet influence of Pleiades?' Honey, that's the group of stars I pointed out once, that we call the Seven Sisters. There's the big star Orion, that some folks think is the seat of Zion or heaven."

Her grandfather reflected for a few moments, looking at his granddaughter searchingly. He took a deep breath and spoke carefully.

"Honey, ain't you a little bit young to be worryin' your pretty head 'bout such grownup ideas as stars an' the circuits of heaven? I used to wonder 'bout such things myself and wouldn't have known nothin' except when I was in prison, when that Union spy had his pallet beside me and told me what he learned in the University 'bout astronomy. A Bible Society outfit gave a bunch of us soldiers Bibles and it's a fine thing they did, though at first we wasn't anxious to carry the added weight. It's all I had to comfort me an' hope for to git rescued. I found out that the Bible has lots of answers, if'n you've got a mind to understand. Arcturus, I was told, is the biggest and brightest star. So it goes to show that the wise men of old knew plenty 'bout the heavens. I wish I knew more, child, but now I'll have to git back to plowin'. We'll talk about it agin sometimes."

Gladys would not let go of his hand as if pleading for answers.

Her grandfather hesitated, then said, "Darlin', all I kin say is hitch your wagon to a star. Then this cruel ol' world cain't touch ya, but you'll live apart from the rest of the world. That may be good in some ways, but agin, nobody will understand ya, ya kin bet on that."

At this she let go of his hand and marched off stiff-legged with her pert little nose angled towards the clouds.

* * *

Nellie, the milk cow, ordinarily was gentle except when she had a calf. In the spring she had a black-and-white bull calf that the children thought was adorable. Papa Jim had warned the young ones to keep their distance from Nellie until the calf was old enough to be weaned.

On this particular occasion Rob and Gladys were not able to restrain Mabel from following them when they had crawled through the lower strands of the barbed wire fence into the pasture to play in the straw stack not far from the corral. Nellie had eaten a hole on one side of the straw stack which left a shallow tunnel where the children liked to play. Nellie was nowhere in sight but she must have been chewing her cud behind the stack, for as they entered they found the calf asleep in their favorite playground. Mabel cuddled up close beside him.

Suddenly Nellie appeared and with eyes ablaze stormed at Rob and his sisters, rushing them as far back in the straw tunnel as they could go, frightening the wits out of them. Their only defense was to throw straw in her face, which also made the tunnel a bit deeper. Mabel, just a toddler, did not grasp the situation as quickly as the others and at first thought that the flying straw was just another aspect of the game. It was only when a horn came precariously close to her that she really began to hear what the others were yelling about, and she too, withdrew back into the tunnel. Gladys grabbed her arm and then her shoulder, protecting the little one with her own slender frame. Nellie stood at the entrance, bawling threateningly at the children. By this time the calf was standing behind his mother, peeping with curiosity round her hindquarters.

"Gladys," Rob said in a shaky voice, "you stand there and watch while I pray. And keep throwing straw at her. Oh Lord, don't let anything happen to Gladys, Mabel, and me. Nellie has gone on a rampage and she's acting like a bull."

His prayers must have been heard, because about that time Lizzie, who had been looking for them, arrived, and seeing their plight, chased the angry cow away. While escorting them back to the house, she was of a mind to punish them for disobeying their father, but seeing their tear-stained faces and their hair and straw-covered clothes, she decided instead that they had had their own punishment.

***

Some time later Gladys had an unprecedented mystical experience, which eventually affected her whole adult life. Rob had gone to town with their father and Mabel was taking her nap. Mother and daughter were sewing when Lizzie asked, "I don't suppose you have any idea what kind of varmint is stealing the chicken feed in the buggy shed?"

"No, ma, I don't but I'll go take a look," said Gladys. "It could be that raccoon that Papa saw once around back of the barn last week. I'll take my skipping rope along."

"Be careful," warned Lizzie. "Take Bugle along to chase the varmint if you should see one."

Gladys agreed, and accompanied by the English pointer, set off to the tack room where the kegs of feed were stored. Bugle lifted his head, his nose quivering as he tested the air. Seeing movement in the field beyond, he took off running.

When Gladys opened the door to the tack room she encountered two benign-looking strangers there who welcomed her in. The elder sat on a workbench and the other sat near the door on one of the kegs. Although these personages were completely different from anyone the child had ever seen and their clothes alien to her knowledge, she was not in the least bit frightened. It was obvious to her that the elder man with tufts of white hair showing underneath his strange headgear, was the one whose interest was focused on her. Instantly he began mental communication with her and despite her tender age she completely understood the heavenly knowledge he imparted. The younger man only smiled in agreement.

The little girl stood on the grain-strewn floor in the center of the harness room with the scent of leather, without a doubt that these superior men were her friends. It even flashed through her innocent mind that they had come to answer her query about the heavens. So she mentally put the question to them. Whatever response they gave her satisfied her at the time. They exchanged messages for what seemed like a long time, but in reality was just a few minutes when they prepared to take their leave. Two ideas that became apparent to her were that their meeting was not to be mentioned to anyone for the present. The other was that she was not to follow them outside immediately. She faithfully complied. The only contact that Gladys had with either was at their departure, when the elder man bent down and touched her in the center of her forehead. At that moment of contact the child felt a surge of warmth, her whole being charged by their presence and manner. They impressed her with the assurance that she would remember them always and that their interest in her would continue. When Gladys thought she could leave she looked up and saw that her strange visitors had lifted up in the air about fifty or sixty feet, then disappeared from sight. She wondered what kind of contraption they rode in, but having nothing to compare it with, she couldn't imagine what it might be.

Although the whole episode seemed quite normal to her at the time, Gladys felt she was walking on air as she returned to her mother.

"What did you find? You stayed away so long I was about to go looking for you," Lizzie asked.

The only answer the child gave was, "Aren't men wonderful? All they have to do is just wish they are somewhere else and in a moment they can be there!"

"What ever gave you such a silly notion?" Lizzie asked, clearly taken aback. "Sis, don't you know if you want to go anywhere you either have to walk, ride in a wagon, carriage, buggy, or ride a horse? Of course once you get to Alva you can take the train and go places."

Gladys felt crushed. From that moment on she knew that she could never share her experiences with anyone with such a limited imagination.

Many months later her teacher at the little red schoolhouse found her crying, with tears streaming down her cheeks, so she kept the child in during the recess. "What ails you child? Are you ill, or did you get a licking before you left home?" the teacher asked sympathetically.

"I can't rightly say what it is, but I feel like my best friends have gone away, far, far, far away, and I won't see them again."

CHAPTER 25

JOSH

Several times when Jim went by Josh's place there were signs suggesting that Josh was not alone. Then one cold day in early December of 1901, Jim saw smoke curling up from the chimney with no horses tethered in the yard. He stopped the wagon and let the reins down inside the gate and walked up the rutty road to the house. Josh's face was covered with lather when he came to answer Jim's knock and usher him inside. He held a razor strop in his hand, with which he had been honing a razor.

"Come on in, Jim, you old mule-skinner! Where you bin keepin' yourself these days?" The two friends shook hands.

"Why, Josh," Jim teased, "I would have never believed it had I not seen it with my own eyes. If I didn't know you better I'd have thought you were sprucing up for some little gal. Maybe you are?"

"I was awonderin' what you'd think of my disguise," Josh answered. "Nobody has seen me with my beard trimmed and part of my face all shaved. I even got me a barber shop haircut the other day, and I bought this here tin tub. 'Course I kin do my washin' in it, but now I'm practicin' takin' a Sattidy night bath."

"That's the caper, Josh. If you wanted to hide your identity you couldn't have thought of a better way to do it. Look at yourself in that shaving mirror. You look downright decent! First thing you know you'll be putting axle grease on your hair, and Bay-rum on your face and smelling like a flower garden."

Josh finished trimming his beard and washed off the remaining lather, while he grinned good-naturedly at his friend.

"First, what's come over you, Josh?" Jim smiled and asked curiously. "And who's the young lady you've taken a fancy to, if it's any of my business?" he added.

"It started, I guess, at one of the places I was ahidin' out at on the last trip," Josh said, feeling a little embarrassed talking about females. His had been a strictly male existence, except for those rare times when in the bigger towns he went to the public baths[1] and ended up in a bawdy house. Usually he was unable to recall very much about the strumpet whose bed he had shared, due to the amount of drinking that went on in the early evening.

"There was this place called The Long Bar at El Reno," Josh continued, "and I hung 'round there several days 'til this dance hall gal got to know me. She's not real young or very purty but she made me feel like a person, not a feller that kept ahidin' out. I'd bin gone several weeks an' did plenty of target practice whenever I got past civilization. I knew that someday I'd have to have a showdown with Gambell, and I wanted to be as prepared as I could be with my failin' eyesight, if it came to a shoot-out. I hadn't seen hide ner hair of him since I left on that sprinter of old man Bevis' and I s'pose I owe it to you, Jim. Coffee and Gambell figured I'd show up at my place first. And all Gambell would need to do is to waylay me somewhere once I got goin' on my cayuse. That's where they got fooled, thanks to you Jim, for your suspicions.

"Guess ya don't know how the little gal fits into the scheme," he continued. "I felt more like a gentlemen in her presence than I ever done afore. She said she was tired a servin' booze to bums and wanted to start her life over some other place. I recall I told her she could come and keep house for me anytime if I ever got out of the scrape I was in. She came right back at me and said she'd be real honored to cook and keep house for such a distinguished lookin' man. But as to the scrape I was in, whatever it was, she knew I could take care of myself. Looks like she was right so far, Jim."

"Go on," Jim prompted Josh. "Your story is just getting good. Tell me, when is the gal coming? I can hardly wait to hear about your showdown with Gambell."

"Hold on, Jim! Don't rush me or I'm apt to forget somethin' important. I guess I never had no woman flatter me much before, but when this gal told me I looked distinguished, I begun to think kinda like a gentleman. I said to myself, what am I runnin' for?

---

1 Public baths: a man could take a bath in a tin hip tub at the barbershop or tonsorial parlor, for twenty cents, including soap and a clean towel.

Who'm I runnin' from? Why don't I face my enemy and have it all over with? And from that day I said to myself: Josh, you aint goin' to run away no more. I'm goin' to turn back to the claim, and if Gambell closes in on me, I'll draw as quick as I can, and if the worst happens at least I'll be with my murdered brother, Charlie."

"That makes sense Josh. Did you ever meet up with Gambell again?" Jim asked.

"Yep, I shore did, in Enid at the Red Dog Saloon. A feller at a poker table next to me kept braggin' about eighty acres on the outskirts of Alva, like half of it was his already. It was my claim of course, that he was talkin' about, that his friend Coffee was takin' care of supposedly, for me! Then I heard chairs moving and when I seen the game next to us breakin' up, I tole the boys to count me out of the poker game for a while and I followed the braggart out. I realized who he was and I snuck up and spoke down the back of his neck.

"Hey, Gambell, I said, that title to the land at El Reno wouldn't look like this, would it? And before he could gather his senses I thrust an identical paper in his face to the one in his pocket that he'd been showin' around in the saloon. He looked at the writin' on the foolscap paper and recognized Frank Coffee's signature at once.

"Well, Jim, that scallywag was so dumbfounded with seein' he had been taken in, that all he could do was gulp. Gambell studied the fake title and said, 'Well, I'll be a gol-derned son-of-a-sea-goin' whelp! Why, that dirty bastard Coffee! If he thinks I'll play his low-down grimy game any longer, he's got another thing acomin'.'"

Josh shook his head, and said, "Gambell just growled sayin', 'Why man, I mighta killed ya.' I tole him, guess you ain't the only one that got fooled. Coffee had me hidin' out from you all along and I guess you was after me too."

Jim stood there shaking his head in disbelief.

"The Lord only knows what cock-and-bull story Coffee tole you, I said to Gambell," Josh continued relating the conversation. "Expectin' us dumb simpletons to shoot it out. He'd get my claim, and yours too, for sure. And of course he would get to keep his El Reno forty, especially if I got off a lucky shot at ya in the exchange of bullets. If we both got a fatal slug, all the better, our signatures on the titles we gave him would hold up in any court."

In an effort to learn the terms of Gambell's arrangement, Josh said he had queried him further, "I suppose ya did give him a title to somethin'?"

"'Yes, I did,' Gambell admitted to me, 'but the swag I got hid away don't worry me none, 'cause the map I gave him won't lead him to it. That dirty crook! We ought to go together and give him what he deserves!'"

"Nope," I says, "I'm goin' to get me a lawyer to straighten out the mess I'm in."

"No hard feelin's," we both said at once. Then we shook hands and I went back to my card game. Next day I looked for a lawyer in Alva and found one. You know the rest. Funny how a dame kin git you to thinkin' straight, without knowin' it."

"Josh," Jim said, "You never told me if the little woman is coming. But first, tell me, wasn't this Gambell the stranger that took away the stabbed victim during the night on the day we registered our claims?"

"Yep, Hank helped hoist him up on Gambell's horse's rump. Jim, I couldn't ask him anything about Sharkey or he would've suspected me for sure. Let dead dogs lie, I always say. And by the way, I don't know when, or even if she's acomin'. Ain't wrote to her yet. S'pose she's forgot about it."

Jim grinned and clapped Josh on the back. "Say, Josh. Come to the box supper this Saturday. There's a schoolmarm coming."

"Why, Jim, you old matchmaker! You don't suppose a dame speakin' fancy language would pay mind to a grizzly old codger like me, do ya?" Josh asked with a broad grin on his face.

"Why not?" inquired Jim while he struggled to hold a serious face. "You're a distinguished looking gentleman now, aren't you? Leastwise isn't that what the dance hall gal called you? Not to change the subject, Josh, but how did your corn crop turn out?"

"Pretty durned good. Maguire and me hit it off straight from the git-go and we're goin' to try our luck agin next spring. Maybe the price of corn will go up. How's Hank acomin'? I ain't seen him since you two came here together."

"Oh, him and Ellie are just fine," Jim answered. "Ellie and Lizzie both are in the family way again. Expecting in the spring, about the same time as the calves!" Jim answered. Then he added with a smile "Josh, you better get hitched and start raising a family before it gets too late. You need some boys around here to help and comfort you in your old age. It isn't normal or easy trying to homestead without a family, if you want my advice."

"What sorta dame did you say this schoolmarm is, Jim?"

Jim grinned while Josh continued talking.

"Don't think I'm entitled to anyone but the kind of gal I'm used to in the dance halls. Now take this Fanny at the Long Bar. She's not a bad lot and wouldn't expect but my rough ways. 'Course I'd have to send to one o' them catalog houses and get a brass bed. Couldn't expect the little lady to sleep on a pallet with a saddlebag under her head, could I? I'll have to think it over careful like. I just got out of one mess, and don't hanker to jump into another one if I can help it. What worries me 'bout Fanny is, if the women folks 'round here scorn her, she could be downright miserable. What do you think, Jim? Do you think it could work?"

Jim dodged giving Josh a direct answer.

"Josh, come to the box supper first. Bertha Bradford is getting to that age of desperation if I'm any judge. It won't take but an hour or so for you to tell if you two could work in harness together. If she's the kind you suspect won't pull her weight, no harm done. 'Course you wouldn't want the kind of woman that proposed to make you over, either. She'd have to understand that she was taking you as you are. If you look as spruced up at the box supper as you do now, I wager that the schoolmarm will cotton to you like one of her truants is drawn to a swimming hole on a warm day."

"Don't be too sure 'bout that, Jim!" Josh said with a sigh, "but I'll be there all right, ready to buy her purty box."

Jim felt his spirits rise as he went home that evening. He was delighted to have his old friend back in the community once more. He resolved to discuss the important and appropriate parts of their conversation with Lizzie that night. Getting Josh to agree to attend the box supper was at least a beginning to introducing him to the social life of their little world.

CHAPTER 26

THE BOX SUPPER

Mid-December brought an added attraction to the regular box suppers to round out the social life of 1901. In November the members of the community had drawn cards with names written on them, for each would bring an inexpensive Christmas gift. "Somethin' useful," as Lizzie had termed it.

"If anyone goes into the cedar brakes for fence posts, he could bring back extra cuttings for a couple of Christmas trees," she had suggested with her accustomed practicality.

On this occasion the women had arrived earlier than their spouses would have liked. In preparation for the holiday the women wanted to make the schoolhouse festive in appearance. They found the tree inside the unlocked door upon arrival and lost no time decorating it with homemade bangles and bows, paper chains and cutout dolls for the children's' delight.

Opal had come with her sister to help. She looked glorious in a tight-fitting waist of red wool with a full matching skirt worn at ankle length. Her high button shoes of calfskin fit her feet like gloves. Lizzie had helped her to sew her costume on the sewing machine that had also stitched the fancy black braid at the appropriate seams. Opal was pretty well turned out, and at sixteen, she felt as mature as a woman. In the three months since Dev had left for France she had received only a postcard. It read,

Thinking of you. Arrived home safe. Father isn't any better. Try to write later. So long for now, your friend, Dev.

A rather disappointing correspondence, Opal thought.

The neighborhood was expanding rapidly with new homesteaders. These newcomers simply bought their land from those owners of proven claims who did not wish to remain there. That night the crowd was larger than usual. When the auction started for bidding on the boxes Jim took his friend Josh in tow. Most of the couples had prearranged the identity of their own boxes and in most cases the bidder managed to acquire the supper partner of his choice. The bids did not usually average any more than twenty cents at most. The boxes brought in by single, unattached ladies were auctioned off last. It was then that the bidding became exciting. Finally the box whispered to contain the schoolmarm's supper was offered for bids.

The auctioneer called, "Now! Here's a beauty, boys! Cain't ya just drool over what's inside? Bet it was cooked with lovin' care, to snare your appetite for fancy food. Look at the purty pink perfumed posy on the elegant wrapped package! What do I hear for an openin' bid?"

Jim pushed Josh in the ribs, but before he could get his tongue untied, someone yelled, "two bits." The next bid came from the far corner of the schoolroom. "I up that to thirty-five cents"

Josh had seen the schoolteacher, but he had not been introduced to her in the rush. "I'll bid six bits to scare off the opposition!" Josh hollered out.

The bidding stopped there and Josh took his box, plunking down a cartwheel[1] and got two bits back.

Opal's box did not come up until most of the others had been auctioned off. Sven came better prepared this time and started the bidding at half a dollar, Fritz bid six bits and Sven topped it for one silver dollar.

Just when he thought he had it nailed, a stranger stood up in the rear "I'll double that to two dollars!" he yelled out.

The auctioneer, knowing his business, said, "You local sod-busters! Ya aint goin' to let an outside feller come in and grab this purty box right out from under yer noses, are ya?"

It was evident then that Sven and Fritz made some kind of compact. Sven spoke up, "Three silver dollars."

The stranger at the rear of the hall called out in emphatic terms, "I'll bid a five-dollar gold piece."

He strode over to the auctioneer, plunking the coin down on the table.

The auctioneer rapped his gavel and said, "Sold to...?"

---

1 A cartwheel was a slang expression for a U.S. silver dollar. Josh bid seventy five cents for the box

supper and received two-bits in change. Two-bits equals twenty-five cents.

"Earl Meneffee," the lucky bidder quickly volunteered. He took the box that belonged to Opal, whose hand was raised to signify that it belonged to her. Ott glared at Earl, since he had been doing a lively business tipping off names of the box owners to would-be bidders without a single mistake.

Jim took Josh over to meet Bertha Bradford. They hit it off at first and he told her that she was a right smart cook. But when he wondered if she could wring a chicken's neck, or shoot a rabbit if need be. "I should hope not," she said indignantly, and added, "that, I consider, is in the realm of a man's duty!"

That evening when the Christmas gifts were exchanged, Bertha received a box of bon-bons, in addition to the homemade gift. There was no name on it but she surmised it came from Josh, though he did not want to admit it.

Opal received a hand-crocheted doily from her friend Tillie Metz, who had drawn her name. Then, another box was given to her. She unwrapped it excitedly. Inside a second plush box lay a beautiful gold locket imprinted with two hearts, and inscribed beneath, *Opal from Earl.*

"When am I goin' to see you again, Opal?" Earl asked impatiently.

"I was just going to tell you that Pa and Ma have arranged for me to go to the Normal School at Alva. But I'll be staying with a relative who will be awful straight-laced and strict. Maybe on Sundays she will let you come. Then we can go out walking around the block or on the school grounds. At least we can talk and get acquainted."

"Opal, that's not what I hoped for," Earl said disappointment in his voice. "But it'll have to do for the time bein' I guess. I hope you ain't got no notions to be a school teacher."

When the receipts were counted that night there was a total of twenty-six dollars and eighty cents. The program committee declared it to be the most successful of auctions.

Ellie exclaimed happily, "Now we can furnish all the extra coal the schoolroom needs this winter and pay for the school-marm's room and board besides. It's two dollars a week you know!"

Jim rushed over to say goodnight to Josh when he saw he was leaving. "Well, I see you and Bertha got on pretty good. Come to any conclusions?"

"I offered to take her home in my rig," Josh half-heartedly mumbled, "but she said that she came with the Wiggins and would have to return with them. Aw shucks, Jim, that lady needs a civilized man, an' I jist ain't him."

Josh put his hat on and tipped the rim so that the wide brimmed hat sat far back on his handsome weather-beaten face.

"Ask Lizzie if I can borrow her Montgomery Ward and Sears catalogues," Josh asked Jim. "I'll be needin' some things for my shack. Guess I'll go home and write Fanny."

"Sure Josh, I'll ask her. Maybe it's better this way. So long."

"So long, Jim. Sorry, but it wouldn't work. I ain't never had any luck with virgins or velvets."

Hank rushed over when he saw Josh leaving. Ellie came behind him, bringing up the rear with the Hartner children.

"Hey Josh," Hank questioned with obvious curiosity. "I didn't get a chance to talk to you and I didn't want to butt in while you had the school teacher eatin' out of your hand. Or was it the other way round? I sure was glad about your last adventure with it turnin' out so good fer ya. Jim an' me are mighty proud that you came back here where you belong. We hope you'll make a practice of comin' to these box supper socials. They's always some unattached wimmen showin' up. Jim says you got a new rig. Care if I go out and take a squint at it? Ellie wants a surrey. Says nothin' else will be big enough for our brood!"

"Sure Hank, go ahead. It's a Studebaker. There ain't no other kind that you can buy 'round here that I know of."

Both men went outside to look at Josh's rig.

"Well, I can see you still have the Bevis sprinter," Hank said to Josh. "How does he behave in harness?"

"In the beginning he didn't take too kindly to it, but with a little patience I talked him into it." Josh said with pride. "I bin workin' with him in harness since we bin back here. So far he ain't given me no trouble. He's a damned good horse, got a smart head on him too. Named right, Century, he's not scared by new things. Fact is it sorta seems to me he likes new things!"

"You tellin' me that? Isn't that somethin' now," Hank said. "Thought old man Bevis was goin' to buy him back."

Hank was leaning against the highbred gelding, scratching him under the chin. Century stood calmly ignoring them, except to move an ear, in one direction or another, or to flick his tail from time to time.

"In the end I told him I didn't want to sell him," Josh said. "That's why I bought this rig so's I kin git to town quick and carry back groceries and things without needin' to hitch up a team."

Then his smile broadened to the point where he could hardly contain laughter.

"Course any day you can come out even with a horse trader as good as Bevis, you'd be better to get up before dawn, so I kept him."

Hank asked about the exchange animal. "How about the cayuse you left in place of Century?"

"Oh, I let the boys keep him for the use of the sprinter. They sure was thankful, don't ya know. Them boys had grown to love that old buckskin," Josh said with pride. "Got to be goin' folks. Got a letter to write tonight."

He waved to his friends and moved off.

Within a month Josh had made the trip to El Reno, where he and Fanny were married in a stand-up ceremony by a Justice of the Peace. She was able to bid farewell to the Long Bar and that segment of her life. Following a short honeymoon trip, the happy pair moved into Josh's claim on the outskirts of Alva.

Jim and Lizzie, along with Hank and Ellie welcomed Fanny, thus setting their seal of approval to what otherwise might have been a homecoming fraught with insecurity for the bride. In the ensuing months Fanny endeared herself to the community and her social sponsors by her amiable disposition and kind personality. She had made a wise choice in her acceptance of Josh, almost as wise a choice as his in his selection of her. By virtue of his history he was endowed with an understanding that a less traveled person might not have possessed. Josh shared her kindness and her lively sense of humor, so that between them grew a firm bond devoid of hypocrisy and based on trust.

CHAPTER 27

JIM

Early one morning late in March of 1902, Jim looked at the Farmers' Almanac by lamplight and tried to read the symbols of the Zodiac. He wished that he knew more about such things for he was sure this would be an auspicious day. As the pages indicated, he had planted his crops according to the appropriate times and seasons with remarkable success. He had become addicted to its recommendations, which he combined with hard work and skill.

Jim put on a tweed cap and sheep-lined hip jacket, for the mornings were still cold. He walked toward the family orchard contemplating the mystery of the breaking dawn when the sky turned from gray to a blazing orange in a matter of minutes. A trace of dew sparkled on the apple trees not yet out of their winter dormancy. Next he walked over to a row of peach trees which surprisingly showed tiny bud formations with a suggestion of pink extruding from the branches. Jim also noticed the early blooming plum trees planted nearby. Indeed, this was a morning aglow.

The sun had not yet risen over the horizon and the sky was still ablaze with fantastic ridges of cerise, the fading purple light extending to mid-heaven. Jim had seen the miracle of nature's renewal and rebirth on that morning of March 31, in 1902, a morning he would never forget.

He walked to the stable close by and grabbed the pitchfork leaning on the outside wall, methodically filling the tines full of hay. Barney, in a separate stall from the two workhorses, got the first pitchfork full in his manger. After filling the manger for old Joe and Charlie, he returned to Barney's stall with a few ears of corn.

He was not as tense as most expectant fathers usually are. He took down the currycomb to give him something to do. Starting at Barney's withers, Jim walked around back currying the gelding's barrel and quarters, talking to him as usual.

"Barney, you old single footer, we've been together ever since you were a colt. Thirteen, fourteen years, I imagine. Someday we both will be put out to pasture. But not yet! I've got a lot to do first and you will have to stand by and be ready when you're needed. Not many younger horses have the high spirit you show when saddled for a sprint. Barney, this morning, God willing, you are going to get a new master. One I hope, who will just have ordinary reasoning, not too smart for his old man, with a strong back for plowing."

Jim curried and brushed Barney down to the cannon bone of each leg. He lifted up each hoof, picked and inspected the underside area around the frog. "'No feet, no hoss', that's what folks used to tell me back in Kentucky. That's for darned sure! Right Barney?" Barney tossed his head as if in agreement.

Despite his pleasure in the extra grooming, Barney kept pawing the straw around as though something was wrong. Jim lifted up the near front hoof again, and to his surprise, the shoe was loose. He asked himself how he could have missed something like that. He attributed it to the fact that he had so many things on his mind all at once.

"I'll send Ott over to take care of that shoe, Barney. Stop tearing up the turf. It'll be practice for him if he's ever to become a right smart blacksmith. It'll be his first paid job for horseshoeing, I'll bet."

When Jim returned to the house, the midwife met him at the door with a big smile on her face.

"Mr. Crouch," she announced. "Come and look at a great big bouncing boy. He weighs nine pounds and four ounces." As she led him toward the bedroom, she continued to brag. "He is already as strong as a new-born colt with lungs to match."

"When did he arrive?" Jim asked.

"Just as the sun peeked over the horizon. Dawn is a good time to be born, the very best," the midwife exclaimed.

Gladys and Mabel, who had heard the wail of the newborn infant had hurried out of bed, and met their father in the hall.

"Oh, sure! I guess we're in for another trial of bawling babies!" Gladys complained.

"Why don't they come without tears?" Mabel asked.

"You wouldn't want another puny child, would you?" Jim asked her.

"No, of course not Papa, but ain't we got enough already?" Mabel answered.

"Well, come on girls, if you want to go with me to see your little brother." He gently inched them forward in front of him.

The midwife opened the door and ushered them in.

"Mrs. Crouch, you have a big audience waiting to see that young cowpoke you just delivered."

The three of them looked down questioningly at the red-faced, bald-headed infant. Jim recognized what he sorely wanted, as Jacob saw in Joseph, someone who in due time would bring him out of the famine of having too many girls. And accordingly the baby was named Joseph.

EPILOGUE

Several years after he proved up his claim Jim Crouch sold his quarter section for $1400 in gold, because his crippled hand kept him from farming efficiently. He moved his family to Alva where he bought a six-room house. His first restaurant, located on the north side of the Alva Square on Flynn St, was set up in the back room of a saloon that had a private entrance. Next he moved the restaurant to the basement of the Alva State Bank on the north side of Court House Square. He later bought the Gable House, a small hotel that Lizzie ran as a boarding house and in which Jim had his last restaurant.

After being in the restaurant business for almost two decades, Jim died in Alva at age 62 in 1925.

Some years later, Elizabeth (Lizzie) Crouch left Alva for California where most of her grown children had moved. She died in Santa Barbara, California in 1949, at age 80.

Opal Bevis, at age 17, married Earl Meneffee, the miner who paid a five dollar gold piece for her supper box at the social. They left the Oklahoma Territory for Lexington, Missouri, but did not remain there long. They moved to Coffeyville, Kansas where they raised their family.

Ott Bevis and the vivacious Milly Snyder, bridesmaid at Lizzy Bartmess and Charley Bevis' wedding, did get married the following spring. Eventually, Ott became a full-fledged blacksmith, but not until 1916 did he venture to set up his own shop and general iron works in Avard, Oklahoma, a small town on the Santa Fe railroad.

And what became of the wonder horse Barney? He played a great role in the lives of the first three children. He became a pet and the children were allowed to ride him. Alas, like all things, Barney's time came to an end. He was greatly mourned.

The Stripper Song: The Golden Girls

We're just three sisters from the lone prairie
The home of the Soddies where the wind blows free
That's where we saw the first light of day
In December, June and the month of May.
We learned to dance on the Cherokee Strip,
Traveled the world, carried our grip.
But we like corn and molasses that you can't git
Unless you go back to the Cherokee Strip.

We're just three sisters from the lone prairie
We've climbed our mountain, trudged over hills
Made enough dough to pay our bills.
California is expensive and expects a tip
So we're heading back to the Cherokee Strip.

We're just three Strippers from the lone prairie
Now, we're not so young as we used to be,
We may get wobbly and scared we'll trip.
But one day, yes sirree, you guessed it,
We're headin' back. Where? Why, the Cherokee Strip!

Gladys Iris Crouch Clark

How to Build A Sod House

By Opal Bevis

After the sod ground is selected (it must contain coarse grass roots), then lay out the foundation lines to dimensions desired on the building site selected. It must be a flat surface.

After the furrow is ploughed (it takes a special sod attachment to a regular hand plow), then cut the ribbons, or strips, in two-foot lengths. Gently load them on a platform or wagon bed and haul them to the building site. Gently unload them to keep these sod blocks intact. Before they are used the skeleton frame of the house has to be roughed in, either with cedar posts, or bark stripped poles equal to 2" x 6" cut lumber, for strength. Lay the blocks of sod exactly like one would lay bricks, every other top layer is opposite to the bottom layer. Start laying the walls. The windows and doors have to be framed in and left open. When the walls are completed then a ridgepole is nailed to each end of the center frame as high as desired for roof drainage. Braces and roof skeleton is a necessity. Tongue and groove lumber is nailed to the rafters, which become the inside ceiling and the outside base. Tarpaper is nailed on top before the sod roof of thinner dimensions is placed on top of the house. After the sod house is up, put in doors and windows.

The Bevis sod house leaked the first year but the wild cactus bloomed along with other wild flowers until their roots filled in the vacant spots.

Opal Bevis Menefee wrote this ca: 1896. Until she married at 17, she lived in the sod home her father and brothers built on their claim near Alva, Oklahoma Territory.

About the Author

The author first attended Northwest Normal School, Alva, Oklahoma while working in her father¢s restaurant. In 1912 she was sent to Wichita, Kansas to attend Mt. Carmel Academy. After returning home, and refusing to work in the restaurant, she took the Santa Fe train from Alva to Kansas City, Missouri, to stay with her Aunt Vena. On the train, she met and later married the man of her dreams, Charles Henry Clark. In 1920 the couple moved to Hollywood, California, where Charles Clark practiced law for twenty-two years. The Clarks left Hollywood in 1941 for the life of ranchers on their 360-acre ranch in San Diego County, California. Over the years their growing curiosity and thirst for archaeological knowledge led them in search of antiquities and archaeological sites on five continents. Her articles on their journeys were published in several magazines and earned her a Eugene Field award for her article on the Andes of South America.

In 1936, Paramahansa Yogananda, the great East Indian spiritual leader initiated Iris, (as she preferred to be called). She developed a deep and knowledgeable interest in comparative religions. After her husband died in 1977, she moved to Sedona, Arizona to began her in-depth study in classes taught by Lehman Hisey on *"The Book of Knowledge: The Keys of Enoch."* by Dr. J. J. Hurtak. When Mr. Hisey retired, Dr. Hurtak appointed her to teach and write on the "Keys," culminating in her book, *"Forever Young,"* published in Santa Fe, New Mexico in 1987 with a second edition published in 1990 in Sedona, Arizona. This remarkable woman, still full of love and laughter, died at 103 1/2 in July of 1999.

Her daughter, Carmelita, lives in Paso Robles, Ca.

www.ingramcontent.com/pod-product-compliance
Lightning Source LLC
Chambersburg PA
CBHW062202280526
45788CB00001B/404